Also by the author

Hazard and the Five Delights

In the Unlikely Event of a Water Landing

Christopher Noël

In the Unlikely Event of a Water Landing

A GEOGRAPHY OF GRIEF

TIMES BOOKS

RANDOM HOUSE

LIBRARY OF CONGRESS CATALOGING-IN-PUBLICATION DATA

Noël, Christopher.

   In the unlikely event of a water landing / Christopher Noël.

     p. cm.

   ISBN 0-8129-2679-X

   1. Noël, Christopher—Biography. 2. Authors, American—20th century—Biography. 3. Traffic accidents. 4. Loss (Psychology). 5. Grief.

6. Death. I. Title.

PS3564.0294Z47 1996

155.9'37—dc20   95-39850

Random House website address: http://www.randomhouse.com/

Printed in the United States of America on acid-free paper

9 8 7 6 5 4 3 2

First Edition

Designed by Beth Tondreau Design / Robin Bentz

To Chris Noël and the Family of Brigid Clark:

I am writing to express my sympathy at your loss, and to share some of Brigid's last hours here. She did not respond or regain consciousness during the time she was with us at the hospital—but I believe each person hears what is said, on some level, until the moment of death. Thus, I did talk to her, explaining what we were doing and that you, Chris, were there along with others who love her. On the way to Burlington I reminded her you were there, waiting for her, of her friends and family who love her, told her her parents were on their way and reminded her of their love, too.

We stayed with her in Burlington for a while—assisting in the flurry of medical activity and getting reports on her condition. . . . I continued talking with her, hoping a by-now-familiar voice would be comforting.

Before we left, I reminded her again of those who love her, asked her to fight as hard as she could to stay with you—and assured her that if the fight was too painful, or just too much, that you, her parents, and her friends, would understand—that you all still love her.

I do not wish to intrude upon your grief with this note—I don't know if you got to see her in Burlington, and I wanted you and her parents to know that Brigid was not alone amidst our scientific-medical efforts to save her. I am so sorry our very best was not enough to keep her with you—

Sincerely,
G.E.
(Emergency Room nurse,
Central Vermont Hospital,
Berlin, Vermont)

one

The split second before it explodes, a bomb will inhale oxygen enough to feed its detonation. If it's in a small container, it will suck at the walls, causing a near vacuum.

On grenade days, as I call them, my chest almost caves in. The pin has been pulled but the grenade refuses to explode; it's just about to. The violence would be a relief. Everywhere I go I go gingerly, because although I do want it to explode, I also want to take care of it before it does, because it's a soft little bomb, very very tender somehow at its center, and as crippling in its demand for constant protection as for its threat.

I can't explain this softness, except to say that it sometimes seems the bomb *contains* the accident scene in miniature, suspended at the instant before impact, our blue Honda Civic only just starting to swerve—as reports have it —out of the way of the Ford Bronco spinning toward her on ice. And the softness in this scene isn't Brigid herself, as you might think. It's more like a point, not physical, but a point of silly, sunny possibility to place

3

against the pinpoint accuracy of the crash (as though aimed for her drowsy head).

It's like this: Soon afterward, my mother dreamed the whole thing out again as a brief ballet, the Bronco pirouetting ardently toward Brigid but halting with the sort of cleanness a halt can have when it seems premature, a millimeter from the Civic, parallel but switched around, so that when the driver rolled down his window (it was a man in this version), he could lean out and lightly kiss the hatch of our gas tank, which he did, then laughed and drove away.

Mythologizing is no surprise, of course, except that it begins immediately, from the moment I walk up to the hospital's front desk, ready to hear she has a broken this or that, and hear instead, in tones of reassurance, that she still has a pulse. I am not allowed to see her because her spleen needs to be sewn back together, and her left leg is broken, and her left lung is punctured and collapsed, all of which are "small potatoes" next to the head injury.

I sit down on the plastic chair against the wall.

Okay, I'll just wait here; I'll be over here. But while I'm waiting could you tell me, please, what did she look like when I just saw her, less than an hour ago, when she said good-bye and left for work? And what did we do yesterday, minute by minute? And how will I dare to tell her this story: "I already felt myself beginning to forget your face, if you can believe that."

I am brought down the hall to a private room, and soon—before I see any doctor— an orderly brings me a paper bag of her things, including the earrings she had on, little white clock faces with blood sprinkled and dried onto them. That'll be good for the story. *Too* good?

Then I'm brought to a wall phone to make the calls: her mother, her sister, Conna, my own mother way down south. "She's been . . . It doesn't look . . ." They fracture like actresses. She, the fact of her, has become, as though by practiced shift, a huge and cloudy notion, a sudden, aggressive brainteaser in too many pieces.

I am still on the phone when they wheel her down the hall past me. She is going to the next ambulance and forty miles away to Burlington, where the head wound can best be treated. She has been stabilized and given seven pints of blood, so I've learned.

This is the last time I will ever see her. She comes out of foggy storyland and then—zip—goes back into storyland, wheeled off through doors that fly open automatically. But for ten or fifteen seconds, here she is, visiting in the air by me, though not pausing. Yes, I could drop the phone and run over, close the distance of perhaps eight feet, make them stop the gurney while I touch her and say words to her, that whole routine. But I'm just looking, thank you. Her face is round and pale, head wound hidden on the other side, eyes closed, hair just as we left it. Somehow, somehow, I can relax. She is so much smaller and cleaner and simpler and . . . fresher than her implications. I take refuge in how she's really no more difficult to understand than a hurt squirrel lying there. And it's pure oxygen to have to think, only, Aw, the poor little thing.

to find her

It all started with a game we called Last Look! Right before sleep, face to face, one of our fingers on the light switch, noses almost touching, sometimes touching, eyes ludicrously wide open as though thirsty for all that can be taken in of a face never to be seen again . . . our mouths open too, shamming screams . . . trying not to laugh. Then out goes the light.

I've always had a lousy memory, but even C. S. Lewis complains, in *A Grief Observed,* that

> we have seen the faces of those we know best so variously, from so many angles, in so many lights, with so many expressions—waking, sleeping, laughing, crying, eating, talking, thinking—that all the impressions crowd into our memory together and cancel out into a mere blur. . . .
>
> Today I had to meet a man I haven't seen for ten years. And all that time I had thought I was remembering him well—how he looked and spoke and the sort of things he said. The first five minutes of the real man shattered the image completely. Not that he had changed. On the contrary, I kept thinking, "Yes, of

course, of course, I'd forgotten that he thought that—or disliked this, or knew so-and-so—or jerked his head back that way." I had known all these things once and I recognized them the moment I met them again. But they had all faded out. . . . How can I hope that this will not happen to my memory of H? That it is not happening already? Slowly, quietly, like snow-flakes—like the small flakes that come when it is going to snow all night—little flakes of me, my impressions, my selections, are settling down on the image of her. The real shape will be quite hidden in the end. Ten minutes—ten seconds—of the real H. would correct all this. And yet, even if those ten seconds were allowed me, one second later the little flakes would begin to fall again. The rough, sharp, cleansing tang of her otherness is gone.

Now add to this what I have come to call the double-take problem. Even when memory *does* briefly pull its weight—giving me a flash of her, say, sitting rapt at her keyboard, face lit amber by the screen, or leaning with astonishing casualness in our bedroom doorway—I can't simply *have* it; I must look away and look again, always find the image hasn't held. This movement is, for me, one of the very worst experiences within grief, this swiveling between poles: belief/disbelief; real/unreal; she is/is not; I am intact/I am ruined, et cetera. Because, although it only lasts a moment, it is earthquake violent and ransoms any gains in solidity I may have made.

Another kind of double take occurs when I forget for a time that anything is wrong, sense only that "something" is "up," is in store for me, and I *wait* for it, and then suddenly it hits—a burst, a stroke. Yet at first I believe it must be something good, come just because of the waiting.

Better to short-circuit this entire cognitive disaster, preempt any double take by simply refusing the *first* take. I gaze instead out into a dull and hazy midfield, enforcing upon myself a shocked unfocus. But this trick has tricked me by freezing, stuck. We were warned our eyes would "stay that way" if we crossed them.

People ask, "Do you think about Brigid all the time?" And I have to answer, "No, not in the way you mean—it's more like constant cloud cover, or fog."

I so envy those around me who are visited by vividness, like my sister Jennie:

> I [dreamed I] was in the house. I realized that she was taking a nap on the living room couch. I didn't want to wake her, so I crept in and stood at the foot of the couch. Just wanted to see her and watch her. . . . She began to stir and then to wake up. I apologized and she sat up groggily. She smiled—she became very giggly at once. . . .
>
> She said, "I'm so glad to be awake!" Laughing and smoothing her hair, her eyes hazy and half-closed. Blankets around her. "I was frustrated to be asleep because I missed him so much!"
>
> "Missed who?" I asked her.
>
> "Chris." She gestured toward the kitchen. . . .
>
> I just watched and took it all in. I thought about how in just a couple years she would be dead. . . . I looked at the blue couch, thinking—she lives here now with him. She is safe and she doesn't know. . . .

Jennie's journal is just one of the shimmering artifacts with which we have built up a Culture of Brigid, have sought to reinstate her among ourselves. A top-notch, widely disseminated museum. And so it often seems that the task before me is to relocate Brigid *herself* somewhere in this thicket of symbols and rituals and eloquence that all of us, together, our friends and family, have so devoutly tended:

Exactly four months after the memorial service, I staged an event at our house. A bunch of us gathered, and for ninety minutes we read aloud from her writing, the readers connected by speakerphone to her family back in Philadelphia. I made copies of the tape and distributed them.

I also excerpted from anniversary tapes she'd made for me, her voice just chatting—commentaries on the life we were living, making sure to record the milestones so we wouldn't forget, telling stories and jokes made up on the spot—and then I copied these excerpts and scattered the copies at Christmastime like winter seeds.

With the help of a friend, I made a fifty-two-minute movie about her: still photos; snippets of film and video; a soundtrack made up of voices from the memorial service; and Brigid's own voice too, from those anniversary tapes; her father belting out Irish folk songs over shots of us on our trip to Ireland in 1989; Rickie Lee Jones doing "Don't Let the Sun Catch You Crying" while we see Brigid and me on the flat roof of our house, trying to clean out the chimney with a huge, long-handled steel brush.

I put the voices of her siblings (all older) at the beginning: her sister Conna, brothers Patrick, Brendan, Brian, and Ciaran speaking at the memorial service two days after the accident. On-screen, shots of their family life. Here is Brigid at four, sitting on a low stone wall in front of a lake, hair much redder then, upsurge of curls, wearing blue coveralls; she is sticking her bare left foot out in the air in front of her, and she's looking at it a little sadly. We hear Brendan, now a father of three, sounding thick, as though he's trying to swallow baked beans:

> I seem to be stuck in a mode where my very best and clearest memories of Brigid are as a child . . . and the picture on the casket there on the end represents the finest picture I have in my mind's eye about Briggie. She was a . . . just a glorious child. She was the first time I experienced that absolutely unquestioning love that you can only get from children; and she was the first baby I ever loved.

"Hello, I'm Bri-Bri, Miss Gragina's brother," begins Brian, closest in age, and as he talks we see their mother, Josie, so young, sitting in a rocking chair on a porch, holding the infant girl; behind her is Dennis Clark, the father, smiling; and off to each side is a boy under ten, Brian and Ciaran, I think. Strained, skim-milk light pours in from behind them all. Then that picture fades into a portrait of everyone looking radiant at Conna's wedding; Brigid is about seventeen now, in the front row in her long, frilly, yellow bridesmaid's dress, a bouquet in her hand. Last comes a naked Brigid, about three, standing in a blue plastic swimming pool in the backyard at the Cliveden Street house; shirtless brothers are arrayed around the yard, distracted by something outside the frame. Brian continues:

> I was talking to my mother the other day and telling her how I think we led a charmed kind of magical existence, starting with the birth of my older sister, Conna—for thirty-eight years or so— and we formed kind of a magic ring or a magic circle that felt unbreakable. I felt invincible. I think it's been broken, unfortunately. But I think maybe some of our magic was needed somewhere else; I think maybe a thousand other magic circles or magic

rings were forged at the forge of creation with the passing of Brigid. And maybe it took one of her hairs to do that.

Forty minutes later, near the end, my sister Becky's memorial service remarks: "From practically the instant I met her, Brigid has been not only one of the best friends I have ever had; she's been a better friend than I imagined was even out there to be had."

Meanwhile, we see video from when Brigid was probably twenty, about the time I met her, when her hair was at its longest; she's in her sundress, the white one with the light blue flowers, and is sitting in a lawn chair out on grass somewhere in Philadelphia, watching and listening to her father and siblings and in-laws off-screen. The quality of this footage is grainy, but her face pierces out at you anyway.

We can hear Becky frequently gulping for breath, but her voice is clear and emphatic:

> She gave new glue to our family when we quite needed it, not that we don't still need it. She has been my inspiration, too. Her presence on the earth, her shiningness, her beauty, her love of things, her sadnesses, her hilariousness, her supreme intelligence, her creativity all gave evidence that whoever makes the world occasionally takes pleasure in doing everything right at once. She has shown me how funny it is possible to be, how pleasure-giving, how mischievous, how generous and affectionate, how alive with love. As George Eliot wrote in *Middlemarch,* one of our favorite books, "No life would have been possible to her which was not filled with emotion." That Brigid cared for me is one of my favorite achievements. . . . She has made even Chris even more glorious than before. The happiness she has brought him for six years would have made her priceless even if he had kept her all to himself.

On-screen, Brigid still sits on the lawn chair; she's focused now on Brendan's daughter Jessica, at two or three, whose arms are full of a soft doll; Jessica marches right up to her and holds the doll out to show; but Brigid goes her one better, taking it, standing it up in her lap, and then starting to hop it up and down. At first, Jessica enjoys this display, but soon she stiffens and reaches for her baby as Brigid increases the hopping more and more until the doll's a convulsing maniac and poor Jessica's entirely nonplussed. In the way Brigid is looking around and laughing you can tell that everyone else is laughing too, and after she returns the doll to Jessica (who's instantly happy again) she pitches, still giggling, back in her chair, doused with earned pleasure.

During this scene, my sister's been completing the Eliot passage:

> "Who can quit young lives after being long in company with them, and not desire to know what befell them in their afteryears? . . . Her finely touched spirit had still its fine issues, though they were not widely visible. Her full nature, like that river of which Cyrus broke the strength, spent itself in channels which had no great name on the earth. But the effect of her being on those around her was incalculably diffusive: for the growing good of the world is partly dependent on unhistoric acts; and that things are not so ill with you and me as they might have been is half owing to the number who lived faithfully a hidden life, and rest in unvisited tombs."

I made thirty copies of this movie and sent it all around, to everybody who needed it. It made people weep and weep. It destroyed them with joy and loss; and watching them watch it, I got to weep too (as rarely otherwise), the kind where it feels like your heart, in its actual meatiness, is striking a wall again and again. Watching set us back, but that's what most of us wanted, to be set back, and back, and back, sickened, or else we'd fly onward, feel "better."

Yes, the movie moves me, even after dozens of viewings; it's maybe the best thing I've ever made. I feel good about our relationship, it-and-me. But this relationship is a usurper, and sly— its wowing force easily mistaken for the specific wind I need.

Where is the Brigid who laughed with me?

Sometimes, I set myself tasks of proximity, like the Her Head Meditation. I used to massage her scalp often, so I try to bring back just her head, to see her face concentrating (eyes closed) on pleasure and feel myself touching the bony bumps through her thick, reddish-brown hair. Have I ever succeeded for more than ten seconds?

Other times, I think, Go back, go back, all the way into the teeth of the original storm; try to experience the accident itself, for once and for all; don't let it give you the slip; pit yourself against it by raising the storm that must be in you somewhere. Rage already, rage! If you can get there, maybe you'll find her, surprise, curled within some cleft in the storm's eye, hiding, tucked somehow where you can slide in next to her.

Lewis leans the other way, though:

> As I have discovered, passionate grief does not link us with the dead but cuts us off. This becomes clearer and clearer. It is just at those moments when I feel the least sorrow—getting into my morning bath is usually one of them—that H. rushes upon my mind in her full reality, her otherness. Not, as in my worst moments, all foreshortened and patheticized and solemnized by my miseries, but as she is in her own right.

I seem stoppered in both directions, storm and serenity, kept from

> that impression which I can't describe except by saying that it's like the sound of a chuckle in the darkness. The sense that some shattering and disarming simplicity is the real answer. I said, several notebooks ago, that even if I got what seemed like an assurance of H.'s presence, I wouldn't believe it. Easier said than done. . . . [But] it's the *quality* of last night's experience—not what it proves but what it was—that makes it worth putting down. It was quite incredibly unemotional. Just the impression of her *mind* momentarily facing my own. . . . I had never in any mood imagined the dead as being so—well, so business-like. Yet there was an extreme and cheerful intimacy. An intimacy that had not passed through the senses or the emotions at all. . . . One didn't need emotion. The intimacy was complete—sharply bracing and restorative too. Can that intimacy be love itself? . . . Brisk? cheerful? keen? alert? intense? wide-awake? Above all, solid. Utterly reliable.

We were proud of inventing Last Look!—an enlightened game, if a parody; but all my life I've had moods in which it seems people must *choose* not to vanish, must re-create themselves moment by moment—strobic moods I talk myself out of, because they are melodramatic. In the Middle Ages, the scholastics said the cosmos is sustained only by divine will repeatedly renewed. Our current-day label for this outlook is occasionalism; we can put an -ism onto it because we know better now.

Early that Tuesday morning, before she left for work, I rea[l] just wanted to stay asleep. She'd cleaned garbage off the kitc[hen] floor downstairs from where the dogs had strewn it, had back up to say good-bye. She must have washed her han[d]

The night before, I'd done some of the dirty work, gotten out of bed and gone outside to move the car off the street so it wouldn't be towed. When I got back to the room, she was peeking at me from under a little tent of blankets she'd formed, blinking quickly, pretending to be in Big Trouble for having coerced me into doing the job. I laughed at her and climbed in. She turned off the light—no game this time—and rubbed my scalp good and hard for a few seconds, saying, "I love you."

Backlit by the window—but not too dramatically, because it was overcast—now she stood by the bed and looked down. I resented how long she stood there, because several times I had to force my eyelids back open. Her head seemed to keep hovering in the sky. She took much greater care in studying me than usual, smiling and smiling (annoying and annoying me—no loitering, man sleeping here!—until at last something penetrated and I think I smiled back), as though this were "take two" of the same scene, a second chance, as though she'd been, the first time through, too casual, hasty.

She laughed one of her nose-laughs and said, "Oh, your hair is sticking up there," reached down and touched either my head or only the hair, I can't remember which.

She seems strangely tall, and I wish I could see more, see her eyes, see *plainly*. I hope I will. For now all I can say is she's just standing and standing here, very reluctant to go.

In Burlington, at the second hospital, the doctor explained, "We've given her strong cardiac medicine, to try to get her heart to pump blood into her brain. But it's not working, because her brain is so swollen and the pressure keeps the blood out."

"Like a balloon?" I said.

"Well, yes," he said. His beard was in the goatee family, neatly trimmed.

"Oh." I nodded. I blinked.

Today, fifteen months later, no matter what I'm doing (even if kissing another woman), I am still blinking and nodding, having only just replied, "Oh."

I wanted to shake his hand (Raymond Carver shook his doctor's hand when he got *his* bad news), to be classy like that, but he trotted back through the door toward Brigid's brain.

I wish I'd kept him out here for a while, told him a few things he'd need to know, like you tell blood type or allergies. "You see, she is an excellent speller. . . . She cares about many more kinds of things than I do, like plants, and quilting, all the breeds of dogs that there are, and spices. . . . When she was a little girl, and her mother would take her places like department stores and pass out of sight for even a second, Brigid's heart would bang. . . . Two weeks ago, she was mistaken for Molly Ringwald in Los Angeles, and she wasn't too pleased about that, so don't you make the same mistake. . . . She dreamed last week that a giant auk was chasing her. . . . She makes up funny songs in the car, Doctor; how do you work on someone with such a sense of humor?"

When he came out the second time and told me no, I did shake his hand.

If I had kept him from going back in there the first time, I could have sat him down and read to him from Brigid's dream journal, 1989:

> I was walking along a dirt road which ran through a storybook-style countryside. Now that I think of it, it was a road which did not fork or intersect with any others. On either side of the road were fences and hedges and gardens and a series of idyllic little cottages and farm houses. I was in an excellent mood. There were lots of farmer/peasant type folks who waved at me, hailed me, beamed and called out to me. I had a pack on my shoulder—it may even have been one of those cartoony hobo packs.
> [Look, Doc, she's drawn a picture here.]
> As I progressed along the road, the odd yeoman would stop me and we'd chat and laugh and lean on the fence between us enjoying the sunshine and one another's company. The people all seemed to be caricatures, with bandannas on their heads and long dresses, or trousers with suspenders, wide-brimmed straw hats and beards. They were wrinkley, good folk.
> [Hey, Brig, we've finally got the man smiling.]

The countryside swept away in either direction from farmyard gardens into patchworky fields and hills. Really absurdly Disney-like. Tweeting birds, rose-covered arbors, etc. I was having a fantastic time, really loving the day and the chatter.

All of a sudden I was done with my walk through this valley. I had gotten to the top of a high hill or mountain and as I looked back over the valley and the road through the countryside, I realized I was seventy years old and about to die. Any minute. I realized that that road had been my life, and I had spent it all casually whistling, jabbering, kicking stones through the dust, laughing and joking with people.

[We've walked outside, me and this handsome young doctor; it's warmish for January, low forties, but we hop in his fancy sports car and peel out, me driving. He asks me to show him where we live, this woman and I, so I take him along Route 89 back toward our house, which I warn him is a little messy this morning. He takes the journal and picks up where I left off. His voice is composed, but I notice his free hand stroking his goatee continuously, all the way to Montpelier.]

I realized that I had really *loved* being with all those friends, but that I had neglected to *write* anything! Now I was about to die, I had maybe 40 seconds, and there was no way to remedy it! I was filled with horror!

That was it. When I woke up I told Chris and he laughed and laughed, it was so obviously an anxiety dream. But now that I write it out, I realize that the Disneyish atmosphere is *completely* comic, that it is also a dream which *parodies* my anxiety, as though I am utterly without will and completely at the mercy of 2-dimensional pleasures.

object at rest

Sixteen months and libido lifts. Suddenly, like a fever that has seen me through. Even as the effort I've just described, to find Brigid, continued, so did sex. Sex was a symptom of a larger desire for life, for knocking up against life and letting it knock back, for trying to believe it won't vanish too, a desire to lean away, hard, from Brigid and her pulling gravity, away from identifying with her by feeling cold, dead, ashes, stone, dust, trembling with a cellular guilt at being able, say, to yawn or scratch my knee or melt butter in a pan.

At the beginning, I missed her like an expert. In those first days and weeks, I stared at all the pictures, read her fiction, listened to her chipper, playful voice on tapes, shoved myself up against what had happened, disbelieving, horror-struck, and wished for all I was worth *not* to flee from it again but to be allowed to freeze there, a Maximum Grief Statue.

Call it an obscene elasticity, then, that let me not only flee from this state but do so with such flourish, to go to bed with five women in the first eleven months, to feel cured by them, by their drama, stirred and glistening in it, *needing* to glisten and swim, craving only fluid (good-bye, Maximum Grief Statue!), an otter diving into pool after pool, all stomach and coat, following every lead he's given, terrified of sitting still.

In *Leftover Life to Kill,* Caitlin Thomas admits to vigorously sleeping around after her husband's death,

> violating purposefully my most precious holy vows to Dylan; saying his golden endearing words for me to them, making the same familiar sweet affectionate gestures; ruthlessly pillaging the long years of our woven heart together; inciting a deliberate sacrilege, a shameful sacrifice of our love. . . . And all this fervour of destruction to no, not one . . . curative effect in my buried, unremitting, black burning world; the ridiculous reverse: an increase in my inescapable dedication to Dylan.

My five brief relationships have worked this way too; though each seemed at the time to contain its own authenticity, and probably did, I now know that most crucially two things were going on: my body was resuming its habit of embrace, since my mind was unable to gain a hold; and I was trying to reach immediately—as in time-lapse photography—what Brigid and I had been struggling to reach together for years: the sort of joyous sexual pitch that Caitlin couldn't give up, that led her even to wish to "ferret down to the long locked cold box, and burst it apart. There to press my headlong hot flesh into his, to mangle him with my strong bones, mingle, mutilate the two of us together, till the dead and the living would be the desired One."

Brigid was the most playful and also the saddest person I

have ever known. Her playfulness is far easier to talk about, was prominent in the memorial service stories. Three weeks after the accident, I met with her therapist, the only person at that ceremony to call Brigid's "deep sorrow" by name. At the end of our session, she said, "You know, you never had all of her."

It's June again, which means I made it through two springs, a summer, and a winter, in our house in Montpelier, Vermont.

I have just moved to Northampton, Massachusetts, into a happy two-story apartment with a long, deep bathtub. My family and friends helped me to empty the house Brigid and I bought and spent seventeen months in—a thirteen-room, cheap, deteriorating, flat-roofed Victorian, 1884. We packed me up in a U-Haul truck and sent me on south.

I decided only weeks ago that I had to move, quite on a dime. I'd holed up dutifully in our house for the dark months; it was dark inside too, and cold, sometimes reaching the low forties by morning, oil furnace switched off to save money. The woodstove, which had, when we lived here together, pumped out heat all night long, stood unused this winter, because I didn't have the heart to buy and stack wood, lug it upstairs from the basement, start fires that would keep moaning, then going out, miserable to exist.

Or the heart for much else, certainly not for writing my fiction. Instead, I'd lie in our bed, on the couch, on floors; stare into space; try to gather my powers of concentration for my job —reading and responding to my students' fiction; watch TV;

eat spaghetti; drink red wine; sleep ten or eleven hours a night; go down for naps during the day; talk on the phone to everyone whose life had been convulsed and beautified by Brigid's death. I often wished I would get very ill, go ahead and break down properly, *be ashes* already. Or else spring back to life. One or the other, instead of this dull region, this nullified sensation, this void that avoids extremes.

That first March, five weeks after the accident, warm air softened the Winooski River and an ice floe broke loose, traveled south, jammed at the bend beside the Grand Union. The river backed up and filled downtown Montpelier with five feet of water. I thought, Good, now all things will change. But except for muddy stains and some structural damage, the town returned to itself. And the floodwaters hadn't reached the crash site, washed it away. (Brigid had taken a right over the bridge, crossed the still-frozen river, then turned left toward Goddard College.)

The first spring arrived on schedule—all that commotion— then came the next three seasons, then another spring, the year revolving dutifully, blatantly, like some rinky-dink carousel.

Our house remained apart—a quiescent museum, all the old angles and surfaces standing mutely around me, and of course the belongings, made relics overnight, overmoment, skirts hanging straight in their closets; drawers full of her balled sock pairs; collected mugs and wine glasses; a set of Beatrix Potter china just given to us by Conna, stacked neatly on a kitchen shelf.

I twisted like an earthworm on a hook.

Sometimes it relaxed me to consider that just as *soon* as the goatee-doctor lost his patient, Brigid's death was already as *safely* part of the past as, say, the death of Socrates.

The house went on sale in September. Seven months later, one day in April, although I'd received zero offers, I knew it was time to go. I found tenants, held a yard sale, ruthlessly junked and boxed, cleared out, and now here I sit—summertime, the start of a brand-new life just far enough away, in a town just enough larger than Montpelier, and just full enough of people who don't know what's happened to me.

And somehow, this external swirl of activity *has* worked, at least, to still me inside; all the bustle of leave-taking and arrival has let me relax; the great museum has been dismantled, so I don't have to muster great romantic melodramas to counter its dead weight anymore.

When I envisioned this new life, it was full of ruddy party-going, of branching out, sashaying forth, clawing after the future. I thought the loneliness of small-town Vermont was making me sick, that, like Aristophanes' bisected sphere-creatures in Plato's *Symposium*, I would now take up the devoted task of finding my other half or, in my version of the myth, *another* other half.

But surprise, I'm core-calm instead, gifted suddenly with the patience of an old man, these sunny June days. Rather than being sick from dwelling in aloneness too long, apparently I haven't even properly *arrived* there until now.

It is a gusty morning, and though I'd rather stay in bed and simply listen to the progress of the world broadcast in the muf-fled sounds of the wind, I get up and take our dog Romeo—a

Shetland sheepdog—to the athletic field, throw the tennis ball for him in long arcs above the bright, mown grass, watch him streak across and reach the ball, over and over, on its first hop. Brigid loved to see him run.

Norman Rockwell lived not far from here, in Stockbridge, Massachusetts, and you can tell. Little Leaguers play catch; folks run with their dogs or push babies gently in the swings; couples sit together on the hillside, legs out, letting the bare backs of their knees bounce against the cool earth.

For a second I picture myself pushing that baby, courting that woman, or else planting land mines in their path . . . but no fantasy gets up any steam. I heard a quotation from Rilke about how the dead no longer even desire their desires.

My mother and I recently visited my sister Jennie in Ithaca, New York, took a stroll by a lake, and it occurred to me how strange a state I am in if even *this* runs against my grain. I understood that at any moment I could sit down—on that boulder, for instance—and stare into space for an hour or two and sense not the slightest restlessness. It's simple: I am essentially an object at rest, and, as we learned in school, an object at rest tends to stay at rest.

Romeo's finally tiring under this sun; I better take him back home, then maybe climb into a cool bath, keep the lights off, swish water around with my hands. Later, I'll see my great friend Joy, a lovely, ingenious woman who adored Brigid, adores me, has helped me through from the beginning, whose town this is, and whom I might fall in love with soon, but not right away.

During the first year, many people said, "You must be writing about this, aren't you?" But no, it's taken these sixteen months for me to catch up to where I am. Just here, just now. In this tranquil Between, then, I'm perhaps finally situated to try to describe a few of the ten thousand facets of what it is and has been to lose Brigid Clark.

As it turns out, there's a great deal of space to study, and it begs to be lavished with attention, and though sometimes I try to feel I'm falling through the billowy-aired rabbit hole, lucky, I know it's not that way at all, no fascinating destination, because it's equal on all sides, this kind of space is, the kind with no objects in it or sound or movement. The walls of my bedroom, the headboard angled by my face, the desk against that wall, the window picturing a world—they are fakes. What we have, what we seem to have is a lake without surface or bottom, bankless too in all directions, which is the only lucky thing, because any limit, even a thousand miles off, would clog me.

Hours each day, I drink it in, my eyes and ears suckling to get as much as they can, but there's never enough to fill me with clean newborn nothing. Vast tons of fresh water, flowing through, haven't emptied me out; I keep secreting the other kind of nothing, like squid ink that will not rinse.

Or else it seems a quiet, endless bleeding out my eyeholes, this blood the stuff of thinking before it comes to thoughts. Thoughts have not been favors for a long time; in a bid for hollowness, I'll send them away, before they can cause further trouble.

Or, sometimes, the lake is a lake of air, and what's in my chest is a thing so rotten—for some reason I keep picturing a cabbage —that it gives off a sickening gas, heavy and reeking, checking my breath, spreading a soft putrescence through my flesh. If I had a box with such a cabbage in it, I'd carry it outside and put it in the middle of a field, let it air out, through and through, all summer long, till that cabbage is dry and light as rice paper.

But there isn't enough breeze to accomplish this.

I have noticed that my eyes tick minutely from setting to setting, as though I'm idly browsing, free, free of focus, surveying some private structure before me just here inside this particular blur. Or am I building it myself from the ground up with these soft hammerblows of vision, a dwelling I can step into full-bodied once I get it finished?

For the first time ever, thanks to my special circumstances, I have this luxury. In years past, I always did this sort of necessary work off alone, in minutes swiped from the greedy world of Focus, but fugitives cannot truly build. The way things are now, I am only a fugitive when I step *out* of Blur and into Focus, when I pretend to be an object in motion, skittish, saying, "Nice to have been here, but you understand I have to be getting back."

Sometimes my eyeballs do not tick but remain fixed for great intervals, so that when they do shift I can feel the air's coolness on their surfaces as it edges under warm perimeter flesh.

I slouch in chairs, I sprawl diagonally across my bed, I lie on the floor, in tubs full of hot water, I lean in doorways. I must look like a neglected doll. Rousing myself the least bit feels like setting foot into a bear cave unarmed.

Maybe I am being rewarded for a lifetime of paying close attention, of shooting my trustworthy beams out through all the turbulence, catching here and there on solid points, like a hand clutching roots and branches, as I'm carried along on the rushing river. Maybe this is where I've been headed all along, to this very lake, to attention's home in stillness.

The thing about being completely lost is the lack of drama. *Becoming* lost brims with it, of course, and being a *little* lost also produces its minor-key background music. But here I am way out past any kind of fuss already, and nothing is going on: no spectators, no music, no landmarks, not even a breeze.

Maybe this is why I seem to need what I seem to be building in front of me, in the casual industry of my twitching eyes. Even I, even wandering, even without sight as I used to know sight, even in this revolt from structure, I must want to see formation, even shapeless I want to shape, in this feathery way. Or maybe this is not yet building; maybe it doesn't even quite represent building; maybe these eyestrokes are only drawing on the air, a design one level more rarefied than abstraction, a pretending to conceive. Or are they the ghost of reading?

I can

"I sat on the couch in our high-ceilinged living room," Brigid wrote,

surrounded by the late afternoon winter light and the shadows of houseplants. I was holding a cardboard-bound book which had a bright, fibrous, shellacked cover, and a strip of red tape up the spine. Only a few days before I had left my best friend's house in frustration. We were learning to read in first grade. Her progress made me so angry.

"It's easy," she'd said, showing me the page our teacher had gone over in class that day. She pointed to the words beneath the illustrations. " '*F*an, *C*an, *M*an, *P*an.' See?"

I decided I would read a different book, my own, the one I loved and looked at all by myself, at home, when no one was watching. I would read the way *I* liked to read. It was the book with the two brothers and the two sisters. In the kitchen, the sisters made cakes and cookies with fabulously pink icing. In the yard, the brothers put a colorful ruff on the brown and white dog and made him dance on his hind legs. When the girls brought out the cakes and cookies, they had tutus on. The brothers put on clown make-up. I loved them so much, and their wonderful life; they were so glossy and so happy! I dropped my head and casually studied the words of the story,

30

and slowly, without really thinking too much about it, I began to sound out the words. And slowly, I heard myself saying a sentence. I was shocked. I stared at the book in amazement. "Mom!" I shouted. I slid off the couch and ran through the living room, through the front hall, down the passage to the kitchen, past the pantry. My mother, at the kitchen counter, looked over her shoulder and down at me, smiling. "What?" she said. I held the two halves of the book wide open with my hands as though I didn't remember how to shut it or put it down. "I can READ!" I cried. And I stood by her side as she cut up some onions, and read the story aloud to her.

In bed, pretending to sleep, I study her face, especially her eyes as they flit across lines of George Eliot, Tillie Olsen, Nicholson Baker; I always marvel at their quickness, at how, sidelong, from my pillow, these two seem not large and blue but colorless, just bellied gel, zipping to finish each page, but the most curious, hungry gel in the world.

I'm easier with writing than with reading; my eyes labor across a page, ache with effort. Though she's never wanted to do anything else with her life but write stories and novels, that's where Brigid labors, pressed down by her standards, feeling that she must purely fascinate herself *every paragraph,* that any book she'd find worth writing would have to be "as great as an amalgam of all the best parts of all the best books I've ever read."

The autumn before the accident, she was accepted to the MacDowell Colony. I was home when the letter arrived; I danced and shouted "Yes!" then called her at work. They were going to furnish her with her own cabin for April, and she planned to get going strong on her novel about Buster Keaton.

I keep watching her face, smiling at what I call the "lemon

spot"—not a spot but a small, smooth area between and slightly above her reddish eyebrows, an area of force where all her cuteness and invention are secretly founded.

She'd rather I'd open a book too, lying here next to her, say the good lines out loud.

Instead, I only want to toss her book aside and grab hold of her, peel off her long nightshirt so we can be Dylan and Caitlin; if I try this, though, she'll only get upset—"I told you I *can't* right now, I'm *sorry*"—and I'll be the wild outcast. Again.

As I fall asleep—any of a thousand nights—I can hear her still turning pages, suddenly laughing robustly, startling, maddening me, sharing a phrase or an image, a whole sentence. I always mean it when I say, "Mmmmm, that's wonderful."

You know how in literature or drama sometimes, a person will see a thing that triggers an entire, very engrossing memory or fantasy? I've always suspected that's a false construct, that the mind doesn't really work this way, but now it keeps happening to me. Two days ago, during a scene in *The Joy Luck Club* in which a man culls from his dead wife's possessions what to take to her long-lost twin sisters in China, I suddenly remembered the shoes, and the whole feeling of that afternoon on which we bought them, how our eyes stung and watered in the wind between stores in Burlington.

Black, high-heeled, fake suede, kind of fuzzy.

It was January 11, seventeen days before the accident; it was freakishly cold, and we were just about to fly from Burlington to Los Angeles for the Twelfth Annual ACE awards ceremony. The video version of a children's story we wrote together—"The Gingham Dog and the Calico Cat," based loosely on the old poem—had been aired on Showtime and nominated for an ACE (Award for Cable **33**

Excellence). It was a crazy adventure—many famous people were going to be there—and Brigid needed new shoes to go with the 1930s dress she'd borrowed. I needed a bow tie to go with my borrowed 1940s tux. Hunting down the right shoes took the bulk of our time until the flight. She knew instantly they were the pair, open-topped except for a black fuzzy **X**—two strips of the fabric—over the top of each foot.

On the morning of the memorial service, Brigid's sister-in-law Kate asked if I'd help pick out what clothes Brigid should wear inside her coffin, even though it was going to be closed. I chose a ruby red and purple floral-print dress (the one she'd recently felt she looked best in), the L.A. shoes, and the left earring of the pair I'd bought her in Paris six years earlier, and these shoes.

The other night Romeo scratched a flea rhythmically, and this gave me back the exact movement of Brigid's foot, most nights. We'd be lying in bed, going to sleep, I'd feel her foot (right or left?) quietly bobbing next to my leg, so comforting that I'd just barely notice it. Once, though, when I mentioned it, she laughed, said she had honestly not been aware of it for years, but now that I'd pointed it out she knew she'd been doing it forever. We agreed it was a rare case of having a clear channel all the way back, unclouded by thought, to the Actual Days of Childhood.

My car just came back from the shop, and they returned the keys with a tag on them very much like the white plastic wristbands they give people in hospitals. I pictured Brigid waking up with one on, finding it cute on herself, showing it around to us, letting us think of her as a newborn. And then of course came more predictable images: her joking with some of the nurses, her being their favorite, sneering at others behind their backs. A bunch of us painting WELCOME HOME, BRIG on a king-size white sheet, hanging it in front across the second-floor windows. Balloons. Her carried in a chair?

Slow way down, though. Draw it out for weeks or months in the hospital, your progress is so laborious. How much you need, around the clock, in ministrations. Do you have any inkling how ready we are, we still are? Do I need to tell you how everyone rushed up here? Myriam flew from Raleigh. You love her, remember? My mother? Last May, she held your forehead and helped you throw up in the middle of the night, the night of Jennie's graduation, which makes me suddenly angry at you, as if you have just forgotten that! Your mom and dad *drove* here from Philly, an eight-hour trip. Your mom called me at the hospital from upstate New York. I told her you had died. They kept driving. Kathy and Eric and Susannah and I met Myriam at the plane, and she smiled when she saw us, relieved to be here, ready to get to work. I just shook my head. Within twelve hours everybody was here, *with nothing to do.* A bottomlessness gone begging. As if you begrudge us our absolute need to tend to you, do little things for you. I want to hold a book up for you, to go and get you a fresh straw, to ask about that noise, have it turned off, to smuggle you a Tootsie Roll or root beer barrel, to remind you of something. That's all I want to do, all the time, little things for you. Clean, modest things. Whatever I do now cries out "instead." And if it's "for" you, it's only *in your name*—a phrase and idea I'm so sick of I could vomit. And the smallest gestures in your name are always ostentatious, embarrassing: the flail of ritual.

Looming in each of us, a mountain made of gold, and beneath

that, a cavern filled with jewels; and though you might think we could spend all this in other ways, transfer it to any of a thousand worthy causes, you'd be wrong, it's just for you. So what do you suggest, ingrate? It's a horrible treasure to have. Yes, I'm rich with it, but it's the kind that poisons and chokes its possessor. You've made misers of us. I can feel it literally, an illness, a substance, like bile actually rising in my throat, sometimes more like a gate, checking and turning back any pure affection for people, for the world out there to explore, good books. In the face of any prospect of learning or moving-toward, there's a particular knot in my upper chest that seizes and yanks me backward. My natural curiosity's squeezed off until I'm woolly and can only sink into default again, staring into space—trying your untried coma?—huge, juicy, heavy cabbage in my chest rotting and rotting.

It's dismal, I will tell you, Brigid. And now for the final blow, the Midas-like nightmare: since you've made real that showy memory-trigger trick, look how random signals from the world send me tumbling back to you, where you still need what I have in store for you—and *behold,* the riches locked in me are increased a thousandfold.

This morning, the mail brings ten copies of her "book," her MFA thesis—seven short stories, a first chapter of her projected novel based on the life of Buster Keaton, and an essay about memoir—which her parents have had printed and bound. I sit down with it and page through. Crisp, professional, final. She intended these pieces to be only the first gesture toward the books she wanted to write. From listening to her so much, it's as familiar to me as the sound of thunder that she never accepted any of her stories as a whole; how much less, then, is an entire book, which, in its very boundness, purports to be a whole of wholes?

But I find I can sort of rejoice at what's in my hand if I take it as sheer play, as time spent in language, as her breathing, if I dip in and join up, if I forget its glossy, world-ready appearance, remember that it's just for us few, and repeat the end of her preface's first paragraph: "I have had to unlearn what my reading and my English classes suggested to me . . . to learn that shape and order come last, and that whim, above all, must dictate."

From her story "Sweet on Ross":

> "What? What did you say?" Jack appeared in the doorway, pale as a vampire, a spatula in his hand. "What the fuck did you just say?"
>
> "Nothing! My God! Nothing." I quickly turned and dropped into a chair, and I looked off to my right, and down, as though there were a low-slung something there which required my close attention. I knew this would drive Jack up the wall; it was a pose designed to expel him from the house.
>
> "Nothing? It was *not* nothing! This is what I hate, *hate* about you. . . . You can't have a normal discussion, you refuse to talk to me, but I know you're talking behind my back, you bitch, I know that somewhere, someone is hearing about it. *Jesus!* You'd rather talk to your*self* than talk to me!"
>
> In my mind, I conceded that this was certainly true. I began concentrating on absorbing the feeling of looking down and to my right—primarily a sensation of the neck and shoulder. I told myself: "You *are* down-and-to-the-right. You are the essence of down-and-to-the-right, and there is nothing but you, down-and-to-the-right, unwavering, past feeling and mind—" and so forth.

But after all, reading her feels strangely *unlike* playing with her; of course the boldness of the letters, the starchiness of the pages between my fingers, the close-set tautness of the lines of print, the implicit metallic conclusiveness of type set firmly and expensively somewhere in Philadelphia, all conspire against the meaning of play, because play is nothing if not provisional. But I also know that the circumstances are working to unveil an authority that was in her all along, which she and I were too restless and revision-hungry to ever quite give its due. As she has become, today, more an author, out of hiding, she has become less my playmate. Maybe if I were to read her letters, a game of hide-and-seek would be likelier.

This whole search must be at least *somewhat* like a puzzle, a visual improvisation, like finding the right distance to stand away from a painting so that it springs to life. I am too close to her and too far both at once; she's too fixed and too fleeting. The artifacts—like her book—are so easily held, have nothing of quicksilver to them at all; and then what's elusive about her (what's elusive about *anyone*, that which always squeaks past our "knowledge" of them and circles around to tap us on the back) is simply *too* elusive in this case. One can never, in the best of circumstances, truly grab onto it, of course, but ordinarily one is touched by it, tagged by it. My main question is this: Am I only bemoaning what separates life and death? Is wanting this presence from Brigid just flatly and stupidly the same as wanting her back? A friend has cautioned me not to ask spirit to be matter.

I turn the page.

> To write a memoir is, I think, to be seduced by the idea of persistence, of a single identity. What, in me, persists? Who am I always? What was my source? ... With the passing of time, with the aging of our conscious selves and the loss of former selves knocking about in the backs of our minds, the image of the grave appears and disappears, a vast, black maw yawning at our feet; the world suddenly looms, is all, and all significance—the past must be examined with a magnifying glass in order to draw every drop of life from it. We all know that writing about life detracts from and alleviates the fear of death. It follows that remembering the past is a kind of salve; memories of childhood (if they're good) soothe us, and remind us that we *have* felt; to shape our lives into

something coherent is to act, be vital, to remember that we *are* here, and do exist. . . . Why am I more fully alive, more engaged by life when I write, and in fuller possession of myself, than at any other time? . . . if I reconstruct the movements of my mind with as much clarity as I can, ultimately I will have a fixed (if imperfect) sense of some portion of my life, a portion which I can claim to know. . . . [The] effort to articulate what it is to experience my being is my chief joy in life.

"Meagan watched them load up the blue and white VW bus from her branch in the magnolia tree," begins the story "Fish Creek, Wisconsin." I remember when she wrote it, as a junior at the college where I was a graduate student. I had just met her. This was the first story she wrote that ended up as a "keeper." I can picture the early draft in her handwriting, with blue pen on white lined paper. She read it aloud to me, sitting on her bed in her little dorm room, while I lay next to her on the bed. Until then I knew only that she fancied herself a writer, not whether she was any good. Her voice had that slight sickly edge that voices get when something is important:

The white and pink petals fluttered all around her like flags. Brian had told her she couldn't help. ("You're too little.") He was only nine—that wasn't much bigger than her—but when their mother wasn't looking he raised his hand and gave her a sideways look like he was going to hit her. So she climbed the magnolia and looked down at them, filing by the bank of pachysandra below her. Her daddy was inside the VW putting everything in a safe place with big, dry hands. He was puffing, and a bunch of wrinkles had stacked up over his heavy eyeglasses. The big blue tent with the heavy, clanking poles had been put in first, and then the little green pup tent she and Conna would share. She liked the little tent very much. (Pup, pup, pup, Puppy.) . . . Brian and Ciaran were riding on the sleeping bags, rolling themselves along the driveway toward Mrs. Splendido's house by using the heels of their sneakers. Meagan nodded her feet from the ankles as the petals shook their sweetness loose and then detached, spinning past her toward the deep green lawn. One of the whitest landed like a flake on her thigh. Settling her bottom square on the branch, she freed her hands. She slipped the thumb into the hollow where the petal had most fiercely hugged the bud it had once been a part of. Magnolia-thumbed, she stroked her cheek, her lips, and the place between her earlobe and the end of her jawbone. High up in the sweet air, surrounded by thousands of cool, soft flags, she heard her mother call her from inside.

Her Buster Keaton novel, "Keep Your Eye on the Kid," opens this way:

> When I was young, I used to lie in the middle of the Wonderland stage at night and lick the boards. Not so strange—I once knew a kid who ate at the edges of the newspapers he couldn't sell. We had to amuse ourselves somehow, I guess, and if you ask me, the dirty habits of children are nothing compared to what they grow up into. Anyway. I used to pick out a pattern in the dust with my tongue until I couldn't even taste it anymore, and my tongue was as dry as a desert snake, and then I'd roll over, spit for a while, and look into the rigging, and I used to think that, all in all, it wasn't a great life, but I wouldn't run away from it either. Now and again somebody would open a door at the back of the theater, and I'd hear them put one foot out as they leaned in to look for whoever it was they were after, that one footstep cracking like a pistol going off. Then I'd hear a shuffling, and the door would whine shut again, and I'd lie on, like a heap of gunnysacks right smack in the center of all that emptiness.

Somehow, here, I *do* feel the wind of her playing at me. Is this because I am being taken into the arms of a novel that promises to open wide and go on and on, because only its barest beginning exists, because the rest is still inside her? My father once said, of a particular film, "It promises more than it delivers, but I love the promising." She goes on:

> Did you never notice that lying on your back gives you room to take pleasure in your stomach? I used to like to spread my fingers over my stomach and kind of seize it and push it around while I looked up at all the scenery hanging there. Things like that remind you you're in the world, and a solid creature. For a time, there was a family of dummies who spent their nights under a sheet upstage. I liked having them there, knowing they were lying on their backs, looking up but for the sheet covering their faces, a bunch of wiseacres like me. And sometimes La Belle Titcomb would come in and sit on the edge of the stage and knock her heels together and smoke.

I have carefully preserved hundreds of pages of Brigid's letters in plastic sleeves inside a large, safe, glossy-red-covered three-ring binder. I expected to be poring over them all this time, but I haven't read a one. I feel guilty; if I loved her right, I'd be bathing in her words. But here's a more charitable interpretation of my odd neglect: unopened, they seem approximately infinite inside that binder, full of surprises, known yet unknown, like a person, unable to be corraled, always a door to be opened onto further spaces. Brigid's fiction and her image in pictures and moments on video, the tapes of her speaking, et cetera, have all become external quantities out in the world. These letters are (1) just between her and me, and (2) largely and blessedly forgotten in their specifics. I've set this closed binder near my bed, and I like it there. I look at it and breathe better. Pure possibility coils inside. What could be more certain than that hilarious, peculiar, and strikingly characteristic slants of thought and sentiment and sensation wait in there and that not reading them replants her soul here in the ground next to me?

Does the same go for the trove of my memory? I don't entirely buy the premise that all we've experienced is preserved in us, but there are times with Brigid that I feel always on the verge of recalling exactly. Many of them take place in the car—the blue Honda Civic—where we had so many of our best moments. I've just now realized how strange this is, since it's the same car that crashed. I guess I've been thinking of them as two different cars.

Once, in winter, we were riding along on the Barre-Montpelier road, and she started up with a song about Gregor Samsa of "The Metamorphosis," a spontaneously invented chant she called "Gregor's Lament." It was ridiculous, but she kept going and going. It was in couplets, if I'm right. I know it took a shamelessly sentimental and superficial angle on the story, as if Hallmark or Disney were retelling it. And I know the point was basically, "Hey, be nice to bugs, they're people too!" Although we both often referred to "Gregor's Lament" fondly in the years afterward—since it was a prime example of the sort of car performance art that she specialized in—neither of us could remember any individual lines. She insisted that this was as it *should* be, of course, because the nature of the medium was to be of the moment, evanescent, unpreservable.

But that doesn't help me now. What if I could bring that back? Or any of her other performances? That is definitely what I'd ask for, if I could choose only one way of being with her. Sometimes, if she was in a good mood, I could prompt her by singing the opening notes from Sheena Easton's "Morning Train." Her voice would pipe reedily, taking up the first eight notes, but only the first eight notes, over and over, piercingly,

absurdly high-pitched and frantic, her upper body bobbing like a puppet's, her mind effortlessly plucking along, imagining outrageous little scenarios and plot twists and melodramatic events, and silly ways of phrasing all of this. Now and then I could think quickly enough to throw in an idea that she'd grab and run with. I'd love to quote some here!

The point is, I want to dance with her like this again. But am I better off unable? If I could reenter one of these times—through hypnosis, say—should I? As with the letters, if I stay outside yet near this place, it can seem the crux of all imagination, the distillate of play and immediacy. The performance pieces seem in their shrine now to have gone on forever and to have contained all humor and all life.

Near them, and near the letters, I can watch over them. In another Kafka story, "The Burrow," the rodent narrator tells in splendid detail about the building and maintenance of his labyrinthine underground home. It has many tunnels branching off, false entrances and secret exits to fool would-be intruders, intricate methods of getting food from the world back into the burrow without being followed, and so on. The relevant part, though, is that down deep there is a rounded chamber that he calls his "Castle Keep," where he stores a supply of his best food, and which he has lined with soft imports like feathers, certain leaves. It's the safest place in the world to him, the place he dreams about when he's not inside it, which is, it turns out, most of the time. He loves it so much in there that he stays out.

> What a joy to lie pressed against the rounded outer wall, pull oneself up, let oneself slide down again, miss one's footing and find oneself on firm earth, and play all those games literally upon

the Castle Keep and not inside it; to avoid the Castle Keep . . . to postpone the joy of seeing it until later and yet not to have to do without it, but literally hold it safe between one's claws . . . but above all to be able to stand guard over it, and in that way to be so completely compensated for renouncing the actual sight of it that, if one had to choose between staying all one's life in the Castle Keep or in the free space outside it, one would choose the latter, content to wander up and down there all one's days and keep guard over the Castle Keep.

no angle

Seventeen months now.

I take long, aimless drives in my car, sailing through gorgeous countryside and crawling down small-town streets in East-hampton, Montague, Hatfield, Amherst. Either that, or I stay inside. I don't take walks. Many of these summer days are bountiful, of course (swollen all over with blinding green and pumped full of enough fresh, heavy, quick air to choke me a thousand times over), and I'm not equal to them, hate them, in fact. I can't take the world head-on. When I do have to face it, I wince from the heart.

So this is why the car is better. Not really focusing out the windshield, except for the exigencies of driving, I glance instead through the mirrors: the side mirrors, not the rearview, because the rear is too flat, too much like looking straight ahead. (Also, there's the danger of seeing myself, which ruins everything.) When I catch the world edgewise like this, going fast, it swirls in there, fields and barns and woods, telephone poles and their wires, stirred and stirring; and then when I slow up, it's calm and calming in there, poured into

47

these deep, oval bowls left and right—the most fascinating soup in history. It's when I'm easing along a random residential street, or parked, that I can take my time and feast.

This glass is tinted slightly blue-gray, so that it seems a partial eclipse must be under way in that atmosphere. I feel I'm peering, *healthy* now, in through a portal at an irresistible rendition of the world, one that grants me, somehow, an instant *taste* for its contents; it's held apart from me, and tilted, just enough to allow me to imagine it even as I'm seeing it, at a good slant (I prefer the passenger's-side mirror and sometimes hunch forward to make its better slant even better). I can't help gazing and gazing. Cabbage-chest clears up; my eyes hop to attention from the first, polish the surface of the glass with affection, as though they've never *heard* of idle staring, take me through into that abundant miniature and fill with a relaxation I'm unused to, a kind that's taut, springy, ready.

I'm grateful, so grateful: it's a coy, cool-tinted performance, just for me, organized around a principle of silent delight, in which everything seems both more stable and more fluid than usual, crisp in its own identity yet free to pursue its desires. And here's the huge relief: I seem to *own* it, personally, although it's animated from within. It's playing with me.

Oh, I see, this is a *takeoff* on a "fine summer morning": those trees full of leaves "swish and sway," infectiously welcoming, as are those stenciled "clouds" against a stirring satire of blue; it's as if the "breeze" in there might smell faintly of ginger.

Cars pass along the street and I see them in the mirror, glinting, cleanly and devotedly themselves, causing me to praise the very idea of transit. And I can even adore homes this way, symptoms of lives scattered around—laundry on a line, a little aqua shirt fallen to the grass; scraggly gardens; rusted mowers; cats sphinxed on porch steps; balls in bushes; tidy gardens; half a sandwich on the hood of a car; bikes heaved over and run from as if explosive—whereas normally, these days, each thing shouts to me that I've lost an entire world.

If I park and keep watching, before long kids will take the stage, maybe stay awhile, sit on a bench and wag their heads to each other in conversation; it sounds garish next to the delicacies of my private screening. Or they'll pass through quickly, raise hands to one another, feet negotiating a choppy sidewalk. So precise, so casual: a wrist flipped in jest; a sophisticated toe-thrust used by the trailing foot to ride this girl smoothly down through space from curb to street; a lonely boy in shorts, leaning against a thick tree—does he *buff* those shiny knees?

I go farther up the block, and in the driver's-side mirror I can watch a girl in a long raincoat (is she crazy?) knocking at a screen door that has a rectangle cut out of its middle that contains, in metaled cursive, "Ninety-five," while set back within the opposite mirror two sisters search an empty lot, the one in the headband lifting, brushing off, and holding up a green bottle that was half-buried in the dirt—it fills with sunlight.

Obscurely, I worry about them. I don't quite understand how they carry on in there, how nourished and daily occupied when out of my sight. They are neither cartoons nor plausibly alive, since those bodies I'm asked to believe they breathe in, and all things surrounding them, have settled into a surprising type of depth, snug somehow in a place between two and three dimensions, and at a distance from me that is constantly receding and yet always near and dear. Is it this that lends it all its unbearable poignancy?

Reminds me how I fall for the world, also, when it reaches me over the fringe of afternoon naps, in the form of distant sounds frisking in the cup of my ear.

I suspect that even if that blue-tank-topped boy, riding his white bicycle down that driveway there, were to tumble onto the blacktop, scrape off a length of scalp, and bleed profusely, I'd only smile and say mmmmmm—the wound would be glossy, the blood, as it flowed, a fancy display, and gracious where it pooled.

Lodged somewhere far down the lush throat of Berkeley Street, I adjust the driver's-side mirror by hand, several squeaks' worth on its unseen hinge, presiding over a calculated increase in fond curiosity, seeking the fiercest angle of all. And sure enough, I am grabbed as if by my lapels—no, by my *lungtops*—and pulled whole into fairylight.

But suddenly, two of those same fabled children—the tank-topped boy straddling his bike and the girl who'd pushed off from curb to street—present themselves right outside my window, immodestly round and tall, fidgeting before an intruder. The girl asks, "Need directions?" She's got eyes like black peppercorns, but instead of screaming, I smile and shake my head, start the motor.

When they move off I duck back into the mirror, but a switch has been thrown and I'm aware of being swindled. All this charm depends on an atmosphere of the hypothetical. This isn't my world to gaze at, no! It's a cruel portrait, after all, of the world as it *would* be had X not occurred.

· · ·

I once lost Brigid for fifteen minutes in JCPenney, and I let myself become worried out of all proportion. I knew she must be trying things on behind some curtain, but aren't women whisked away without a trace all the time, never to be heard from again? During those minutes I was guardedly afraid, but I really felt the brunt of it—what it would be like to lose a person in her entirety—only after she showed up, trailing a chosen skirt from her forearm.

Near misses are justly famous for conjuring a huge response, later. After avoiding an accident—during which avoidance we are businesslike, absorbed—we find an impressive tree of horror branching and blooming within us, prickling along our pathways. Looking back, from the other side, we get a pretty clear view of how things could have been different, what they "would" have been "like." A sharp and powerful experience of what almost happened, not despite but *because* of the hypothetical angle.

That's the angle I need. I've got no stance. The truth faces me so squarely it blocks the light, comes at me flat, with no edge to cut me right. Or say it this way: I'm deprived of the backward glance, to catch the receding; the whole broad front hull of it is always looming over me, like a lover without subtlety, without winks and poses, without variety, with no interest in showing off, letting *me* get into the act.

So I have no idea what losing Brigid "would have been like"; in the light of that conditional, I think I could know my condition. But "is" is invisible.

· · ·

The night before, she took a long, soaking bath, extra hot. Some of the time I sat and talked with her. I wish I could remember our exact conversation; I do know she was feeling unusually optimistic, lying there contained by the water, the tub, the bathroom, warm, contained by the house, by plans she was making to leave her job at Goddard in the spring, to devote more time to her fiction writing.

I believe she laid a faded green washcloth on her belly, where it stayed. On another such evening, while I sat on this same low stool beside the tub, she told me that her first sexual sensations as a girl came from her putting a wet washcloth like this on her naked front, and that she must have been mighty young because the cloth covered her all the way from her nipples to her thighs.

But this night we just chatted. Earlier, she'd made dinner for our friends Scott and Jennifer—her famous lemon chicken. We'd all shuddered and laughed as I read aloud from *People* magazine about the young man in the Midwest whose arms had been torn clean off by a farm machine and who had sat in the bathtub so he wouldn't get blood on his mother's carpet.

She and I loved stories like that.

Then, she was safe in this deep bathtub, afloat.

Nine hours later—to the other end of the spectrum: out on the road, out, all the way out, pried loose, worked over, clothing now fabric being torn away. Quite a crowd gathered, I hear; official photographs were snapped that I guess I'll never see. Backdrop: cold January pavement. Just anyone could look, and she couldn't even cover her legs.

I say all this, but I still can't begin to realize it, not the broad, straight story of it. The same is true of the impact itself. It eludes me, it is *supposed* to elude me. It's not given to us two alike: her job was to get it all at once; mine is to take it, meted out little by little, for life.

I can sort of relax when I talk to myself like this. I claim handicapped parking in my mind. I'm as unable to take in the whole thing as if asked to eat one of those sidewalk slabs of concrete. People don't operate that way, foolish to try.

But then there are apertures—into the idea, for instance, of impact:

Four days before, she walked into her dark writing room and banged her nose hard on an arm of the cheap exercise machine I'd bought her for Christmas. She yelled at me for not putting it away more carefully. I ran and held her nose. What an insult, I thought, to hit one's *head*.

My sister Becky waited months to show me what she found while leafing through Brigid's date book, which had been down inside the shoulder bag on the passenger seat: a tiny chip of clear windshield glass driven between two pages. At first she'd thought it was a jewel.

two

T o my chagrin, I have become fascinated by the personals section in the *Springfield Valley Advocate,* by the simultaneous anonymity and shoddy attempts at specificity. I laugh and cringe at the phrases that rise up to me, at the clichéd "Miss Lonelyhearts" poignancy, and yet at night, while I twist in bed, they echo as if authentic.

> . . . leggy . . . Bright & Beautiful . . . seeks hugmaster . . . Are you special? Do you seek beauty . . . full-figured, bored senseless . . . Academic Warmth . . . kindred spirit . . . is dominant, yet still caring . . . not bald . . . challenge me! . . . attractive white widow . . . soulmate sought . . . and like to cuddle . . . kid-at-heart . . . You have great body, too, please . . .

I place an ad of my own. A deep, well-modulated robot voice takes down my words, and it's humiliating, because I'm trying to poke fun at the form of these little texts, to indicate connotatively what sort of person I am, but all of this escapes the voice. In monotone, it repeats after me: "Oh sweet Lordy [capital *L* on *Lordy?*] I should say so." **57**

It takes the voice three tries to understand that I'm saying "lithe," not "live," not "light."

My friend Jennie used to think that having your mouth washed out with soap meant you'd lose it, as when a *road* gets washed out. In fifth grade, a teacher told me that a person can only bend their arms and legs so many times before they'll lock up forever, so I went around very stiffly, saving myself for later. As a result, I'm still lithe at 32. I'm a fella, fiction writer and teacher . . . and cute? Oh sweet Lordy I should say so! Please call with *your* childhood misconceptions!

To write a memoir is, I think, to be seduced by the idea of persistence, of a single identity. What, in me, persists? Who am I always?"

Since relocating here in Northampton two months ago and learning how to lie suspended in this lake of space, rinsing and rinsing and rinsing myself until the day I am pure enough to receive Lewis's "shattering and disarming simplicity . . . the impression of her *mind* momentarily facing my own," I've found it's been quite effortless to feel myself a single, simple entity, persisting on this planet for the sake of approaching Brigid. But it's nearly autumn now, the planet shifts, and in me, again, the unwelcome whispered suggestion, "Move along, young and healthy man!"

I *want* to persist as you know me, Brig, to be recognizable, always, to us; but the obverse side of this stillness is nullity, the cabbage in my chest spreading damp plague-juice all inside me; so I won't drown, I find myself surreptitiously starting to paddle toward the future. This means toward Fiction and toward Eros. But what I'm trying to write— 59 a comic horror novel—is a doughy morass, not the lighthearted romp it's supposed to be, to rescue me from myself, to make me laugh. And so instead the sexual daydream machine is tooling up, whirring and hungry for more fuel, reminding me horribly, in its insistence, of that gleaming-steel, efficient-pistoned machine called STILL TRUE that we who'd lost Brigid found ourselves envisioning last year—how it worked away moment upon moment, round the clock, greeted us in controlled, sleek violence morning after morning, so emphatic that we almost had to admire it.

Well then, why not make this new machine outperform the old? In its raring, maybe it will throw off answers like sparks, warming me to my new life, move me forward.

It hits me one night, for example, like a loud, saving edict: In Addition to the Union Between Brigid and Me, There Must Also Be a Separation, *Now As Before.* All I Have To Do Is Find It, Clean It, And Pry At It With All My Strength. Simple!

But later, on the way to sleep, I think of her-thinking-of-me-wishing-to-touch-me; at the same time, I touch *myself,* idly, with two fingers, brush the skin over one of my ribs. Suddenly, I feel entirely known.

Back in May, three months ago, at my tenth college reunion, I bumped into a woman whom I'd never known but had had a crush on from afar. We had fun talking, and I was still attracted to her. All summer we've exchanged playful letters and joke gifts. Though we live at opposite ends of the state, we keep loosely vowing to get together for a drink. She plays polo.

In the other direction lies Albany, New York, and living there is my friend's ex-lover, a single mother of a seven-year-old boy and reported to be both lovely and a bottomless pool of kindness and cheer. For months, I resisted calling, because, hey, aren't I supposed to be digging my own pool in myself? Finding a hidden spring?

It was distressing, though, finally speaking with Albany, and merely because she has the voice of a particular person rather than an ideal. What would an ideal sound like? I remind myself: Do not ask spirit to be matter.

I will probably drive the eighty-four miles to meet her, because even being distressed by particularity is a favor, jostling, reforming me a little.

I feel these days like the set of a Japanese monster movie, the twilit plateau on which they play out their climaxes, but instead of Rodan versus Mothra, it's Ovid versus the Buddha: the latter's clear, attentive vacancy—seeing through the shifting illusions of this realm to what does not change—being set upon fiercely from behind by Ovid and his zeal for shape-shifting. The white-haired, Roman-nosed poet takes the portly knower by the throat, and when he refuses to fight back—when he'll only stare into space, his eyeballs ticking minutely—shakes him and shrieks the opening sentence of his *Metamorphoses:* "My purpose is to tell of bodies which have been transformed into shapes of a different kind!"

One morning, I receive in the mail a strange white sphere—a polo ball, I realize. And on it, in Magic Marker, is written, "Your place or mine?" and the phone number of the woman from the reunion. This is in response to my last note, which asked, "Are we or aren't we going to get together?"

I hold this ball in my hands as I watch the television show *Rescue 911*. Brigid and I used to watch it faithfully each Tuesday night at 8:00. In it, ordinary people suddenly fall into the most unspeakable tragedies. We thrilled at their narrow escapes, astounded afresh each episode at the tenuousness of life, looking at each other and misting over with full hearts when, say, the burly paramedic would describe, holding back sobs, his rescue of the little girl from the burning car, or when the young boy would tell how he called 911, then waited, held his mom's hand while she nearly bled to death from a stab wound. Phew—close call! How we loved life as prismed through these reenactments and voice-overs, not just for its fragility but for how it always seemed to find a way.

I haven't watched the show once since the accident, because of course I knew I would want everybody to perish. But tonight, lying on my living room floor with all the lights off, sobbing on the dirty carpet, I surprise myself by rejoicing when the boy who has nearly drowned in the swimming pool emerges from his coma. And I agree entirely—nodding like a simpleton—with his mother, who screamed, when she dragged him out of the water, "He can't die!"

Now, polo balls, it turns out, are made of an unrecognizable substance—kind of like wood, kind of like supercompressed Styrofoam, but not too much like either. This strangeness was frankly titillating back when the mail arrived; it's just such quirks that may rescue me, tear the roof off this fetid tomb I have been spending my time in and let a gigantic, rushing, fresh wind sweep me out into new atmospheres entirely. I thought, I'll call the number on the ball this very night!

But just now, at thirty-two thousand feet, a chunk of meat has become lodged in the windpipe of an eighty-nine-year-old man, his wife telling a flight attendant that he doesn't seem to be breathing. Luckily, two doctors are on board and perform a tracheotomy to save him. Two years later: he and his wife walk along a country road in their native Yorkshire, England. There's no end to how Brigid would have adored these two, walking slow like this, helping each other along over pebbles, under clouds. His voice in the background shakes with gratitude as he tells his side of the story.

(On the bookshelf near me, where I have retired the unearthly ball, it has a sickly glow. I feel like opening the window and hurling it as far as I can.)

"I said to myself, 'Well, if this is dying, then there's really nothing to it.' "

An acquaintance told me last year that she herself had once nearly died in a crash. While it was happening, as she flew in slow motion through the air, able to see with striking clarity one pen also flying but poised before her face, she heard a voice moving through her, saying, "It doesn't matter, it doesn't matter, it doesn't matter." She knew it was true. Not that those who love her wouldn't grieve horrendously if she died, but that, from a perspective she was now instantly afforded, it really didn't matter whether she died today or many years from today. And she told me that her life didn't exactly flash before her eyes but that all she was came up through her, and that she was ready for it to. I said to her (and she agreed), "It seems like we're just built this way, able at a moment's notice to take our life as a whole, hold it in our hands like a sphere, let it go."

I was born there but haven't really been there; we moved away when I was less than five months old. In a recent dream, I am led by a male guide to Billings Memorial Hospital. Inside, there is an archive of videotapes of all births, and next thing I know, alone now, my own birth-tape in my hand, I am trying to insert it into a slot at the side of a television monitor. The tape is black and shaped like the enemy ship from *Star Trek*, like a manta ray. It won't go in the slot, so I keep forcing it until it breaks. I understand that my birth scene is still intact inside there, but I won't be able to see it.

On snowy days in Vermont, especially on the dirt roads, it sometimes takes several attempts to make it up a long hill: carefully back down to the bottom . . . get a good running start . . . try again.

My mother has lent me her daily record from when I was born, when I was small. It has a sturdy red cover and lined pages, which I've been obsessively poring over, giggling and crying, nourished by this clean return to my beginning:

April 25, 1963:   Sometimes around other people I get so choked up with love for him I have to look away. Yesterday he discovered the world of ants.

May 9, '63:   Tonight Chris was so exhausted from all his exercise today that he had trouble going to sleep. We were having a wonderful breeze, rain and thunderstorm, so he sat up on the shelf thing and I sat on the trunk with my head in his lap and he just pinned it there with his arms. Very enjoyable.

September 14, '63:   I think [these last] 5 weeks . . . I've been closer to Chris than ever before, and perhaps ever will be again . . . every morning . . . he climbs in bed with me for a few minutes. Then we get up and go out and have breakfast together and then clean up a little and set out on the daily projects.

September 18, '63:   I got a telephone and called him [from the hospital, where she had given birth to Becky]. . . . He said, "Mommy, want a tater chip? A kay," and I could hear it crunching into the receiver.

January 1, '65:   Time oozes by. . . . Chris put his arms around me and said, "My hero!" The other day I did some little thing for him and he said, "What can I ever do to repay you?"

July 15, '65:   Chris has been calling me at work lately. Today he asked me why I answered the phone "Drew University Center, Mrs. Noël" instead of "Mommy's here now."

Polo Ball is due to arrive between one and three on a hot Sunday afternoon. We have planned to go swimming at an ancient set of rock pools sculpted smooth by a glacier.

From one until four fifteen I sit on the couch, unable to read or concentrate on the TV's baseball game. I can only note that same old expansive stirredness brought about by last year's flings, and, simultaneously, an utter thinning down, a starvation or strangulation, not because she is late but because she is coming.

Once, when Brigid and I were first together, she took my face in her hands, held it in front of her, and said, eyes sparkling with a genuine dread: "It's so weird, a *whole person!*"

Anyone honest will admit to having been made slightly but unmistakably nauseated merely by the weight and extent of even a dear one; it's the underbelly of that famous transcendence of self made possible by loving another; it's the *tedium* of otherness; it's the mood you get into when even the way they drink a glass of water seems selfish. Over there sits an entity, implacable, self-satisfied, like a dead tree stump on the far side of a sharp valley, just drily *there*. Whatever's not me is always partially an affront. And these days, when that other is also not Brigid . . .

Sitting and breathing the minutes by, shrinking here on the couch, I remind myself of my grandmother, Ruth Lane, who, lying in bed with pneumonia in the middle of the night thirty-four years ago, lungs filling up, marked her gradual drowning by telling herself, "Now your breath is as thin as a coat thread . . . now it's as thin as a linen thread . . . now as thin as a silk thread . . ." until her sister (a nurse) happened to check on her, gave her a shot of penicillin.

Well, isn't even *this* something to be grateful for, a more vivid and *contoured* nullity than if I hadn't called Polo Ball? It's the *null* nullity that I want to burst free from, the absence that gets away with simply repeating itself blankly, that has no story to tell.

Here's the story. Polo Ball finally arrives, and of course the sparks thrown off by our oblique all-summer flirtation are smothered instantly by the bluntness of proximity. We're polite, trying to ride through to some genuine level, heading off to the glacier-formed swimming site.

Almost all the conversation is my asking her questions about herself, to fill up the dead air, and her answering well and amusingly. Even though she knows, generally, what's happened to me, she never once asks how I'm faring, what it's been like; and even though I can understand why a virtual stranger might shy away from the subject, this disappoints and angers me nonetheless.

By the time we get there, it's pouring down rain, and we have to turn around.

We go out to dinner in Northampton. She tells funny stories and tells them well.

She still doesn't ask about me, once admitting, in passing (as a message?), that in general she has trouble with sincerity.

Are people either pools, like the Albany woman, or wry-edged, like this one? Wet or dry? Is that why the rains came before we could swim, to prevent her from diving into an alien element? Look how everything can seem—when one's own true essence is in question—like an elaborate dance of essences!

Yet (a) Brigid made fun of people and of life itself so sharply —I wish you could hear her—that now it seems the world and its inhabitants are getting away with murder; and (b) there was no limit to her sincere embrace of me.

Am I asking too much?

She accomplished it all without effort, though.

Anyway, Polo Ball stays till after eleven, and though I am perfectly sweet, and so is she, and we have a brand of light fun together, when she goes out the door and gets in her car right in front of my living room windows, even before she starts up I turn off all the lights in here.

Next morning, it's cloudy and cooler, and I find that in my small bedroom there is so much more space to study with my ticking eyes that I've got years of work cut out for me.

All day long, there is a pain radiating from a point behind my sternum. Everybody always considers me to be "in pain," although I don't know it that way. But today I have pain worthy of the name, pain with substance, the kind you can sink your teeth into and eat. I don't seem to ever sob, so I'll take whatever I can get; instead of brimming out of me, here is life at least lancing in, making a hole. Maybe more demoralizing dates will serve as "an axe for the frozen sea within," as Kafka said a book should be.

In Toby Talbot's *A Book About My Mother:*

> Once my daughter Nina at the age of four was weeping bitterly. In trying to comfort her, I brushed the tears from her cheeks. Her sobs immediately converted into an angered outcry: "Give me back my tears!"
> Mourning has its ways. As Ovid said, "Truly, it is allowed to weep. By weeping, we disperse our wrath; and tears go through the heart, even like a stream."

Except that my sternal pain is no stream, nor does it break up my frozen sea. There is no breaking apart, breaking down, no breaking through.

My mother's college roommate, Bette, became a widow when, at age twenty-six, her new husband's throat closed up during Kennedy's Cuban Missile Crisis speech. Every day, all the way to work on the train, and home again, this woman would sob. After about a year, one day she did not sob, and soon she began dreaming about Tony. And she dreamed copiously.

My grandmother survived not only her pneumonia but my grandfather, who had cheated on her for many years and treated her poorly in other ways too. In the middle of the night, less than a year after he died, she was awakened by his six-foot-four, two-hundred-and-twenty-pound body crawling into bed with her. She lay on her side, and he came up behind her to huddle against her back, where he sobbed and sobbed, terrifying her.

I can get by on much less. I'm only asking for an unfolding inside that shows me a way back and a way onward.

"the mouth of truth!"

The snowball explodes quietly against the black tree trunk.

I must be about three. The air smells of winter and it's the middle of the night. My mother has gotten me out of bed, very late. Madison, New Jersey, 1964. We must have crossed the street in front of our building, though I don't remember crossing, because here we are, among trees. She helps me make a snowball, or rather, this she *must* have done. And I don't know if she throws the snowball or I do. All I can remember is seeing it explode and spread white powder against that black trunk. She is standing above and behind me. Her presence is huge and dark and warm and steering. It seems to me now that my consciousness burst open with the bursting of that snowball. But that's it; the memory clicks off.

My memory is, as I have said, not good. I've often thought of entering hypnosis just to recapture my childhood. To my sister Becky you can say, "Okay, it's autumn and you're seven," and right away she can tell you half a dozen separate stories, not snapshots; they're whole unfolding narratives.

Well, I do have a couple like this. Both are set in my favorite place.

I was five or six, and we lived in a small stone house in Martins Creek, Pennsylvania. The Kecks' house, a much larger stone building, stood across a thin driveway from us at the edge of the forest. To one side ran a railroad track, which soon became a trestle with little secret rooms to jump down inside of if a train came over. The Keck boys—especially Timmo—showed me these rooms and explained that tiny people lived in them.

Behind the Kecks' house ran a small river, which flowed beneath the trestle and curved through the forest to reach them.

There were always cats and kittens around, so one day I strolled over into their yard and picked up a small specimen, carried it down to the soft riverbank, knelt, dug a hole with one hand, and then tried to fit the kitten into it. The kitten didn't want to go, splayed its legs out, so I folded them up and pressed it down in, then scooped other mud over to make up for the hole's too-shallowness. At last, the kitten's nose alone poked out at the sky, and I pushed it under, plopped more mud on top, stood up, backed away, folded my hands together behind me, and observed. In a few seconds, the animal erupted with such force that it tumbled into the water and was carried along the surface by the current. I stepped to the edge, hands still folded behind my back, and watched it spinning, blurry, now and then a paw or the head sticking out, like a cartoon character in a fight. Eventually, it pulled itself out by a tree root.

Next thing I remember, Mrs. Keck is after me and I'm hiding, behind trees, in doorways, and finally underneath the Kecks' huge gray car, pressed down in the gravel, bare elbows hurting. I see her thick legs stop right in front of my face; she must be wearing a skirt, because the image of the tiny dots of stubble on her shins and calves is vivid. And I'm thinking, You don't even know I'm here, but I can *count* your ugly hairs.

Next, I am walking down the train tracks; just before getting to the trestle, I veer off up an embankment, into a little glade where I have gone before, to think. I sit here in the sun for a long time, letting mosquitoes land on my hand and fill up, until they are round and translucent with my blood. They can hardly fly away, but I let them. The blood in them is lovely in the sunlight.

Then my mother finds me and walks me back along the tracks toward the stone house, her arm around my shoulders. She says, "Chris, I know you didn't mean to *hurt* the kitten."

It is raining, and Mom returns from the grocery store; the brown bags get soaked between the car and the door. She puts them on the kitchen counter and tells me she's brought me a surprise.

(Same stone house. Same kitchen where, sometimes, at the table, I have grown-up conversations with Mom, we sip tea together in the afternoon, I, dressed up as a lady friend of hers, in earrings and necklace and one of my grandmother's wigs. For these tea parties, my name is Eara.)

I love Gumby and Pokey on TV, and now she pulls them out, bright green and bright orange, held to their cardboard sheet by clear molded plastic. I am so happy. It's the first time I remember understanding that someone can *choose* to be generous.

I rip them open and start trying to bend them into positions.

This is the primary fun, making up stories for them to star in and bending them into different positions. But they won't bend! We discover there's no wire inside. Mom shows me on the cardboard where it says they are erasers. She's so sorry. I keep trying to bend Gumby's arm anyway, but soon it crumbles at the elbow.

Ever since, Gumby has been the name in our family for that very particular feeling, in the recipient, of a kindness that misfires. Down through our history, this has been an astonishingly durable, indispensable concept.

My mother made the world for me. My father and sisters all helped, of course, but she's the one who made it when it was still nothing, and so was I. My knowing of it, and of myself, were made possible by her, which sounds bland and abstract compared to how it is.

The best thing anyone ever said to me was this, and she has said it often: "Oh, Chris, I could write a book about you."

I want to make someone's world, to start history all over again. I feel dry through and through, just waiting for the water of that chance.

Which can be awkward if, say, you are on your way to Albany to visit the woman rumored to be a bottomless pool of kindness. She has a seven-year-old boy named Nicholas and wants more children.

After almost two hours, I arrive and meet them, and she's sweet as can be, even pretty, with striking eyes, but somehow it's immediately crystal clear she's not the one.

For the rest of the afternoon, we go to a spectacular state park

outside the city. It's a cool, fall-like afternoon. I've brought
Romeo (a.k.a. Romers), and the four of us take a long trail in
and amongst high cliffs and fascinating caves. Nick, who looks
just like Macaulay Culkin only minus the big, floppy, red lips,
takes every detour available, trying little rock-climbing forays.
It's obvious to me that I could easily fall in love with this boy
and with mother-and-son. Here is a shape just aching for the
extra piece, and here am I, aching to be that piece. A rich,
world-making life would unfold.

Once, Nick jumps off a rock face backward and lands in the
dirt four feet below. His mother is unnerved, so he tells her he
meant to do that, and furthermore, he says he "timed it." When
that doesn't calm her down entirely, he says, "I *did*...I *sched-
uled* it."

He reminds me so much of myself. And his mother is as
absorbed in him as mine was in me. Many days, she tells me,
they play together for hours. I wonder if she keeps a record too.

March 29, 1965:   C. and I were talking in bed and finally he said,
"We've been fighting the sleep, let's just take it
now."

July 2, '65:   C. says 7-Up is a burglar because it steals thirst.
When he wants more milk he says, "Do you see a
bump on my head?" That means he's growing horns
because he likes milk so.

February 4, '66:   Today C. said, "I'm going to say something to this
day but not to you, so don't get mad. Now remem-
ber, 'cause it's a bad word, I'm not talking to you.
All right. 'You stupid day!' Whew! I'm glad that's
over."

Nick goes twenty-five feet into a narrow cave, too narrow for us grown-ups, and my dog follows him in. We can hear him way back in there, startled, having thought he was alone: "Oh, Romers, I'm glad it's just *you*."

Near the end of the trail, his mother and I are hungry and it's getting dark, but Nick's curiosity hasn't ebbed. He's pulling himself up a mossy slope, his mother says *enough*, and he calls back, "Don't worry, this isn't mountain climbing"—he stretches out along the moss—"it's more like mountain re*lax*ing."

At the very end of the trail, we stand at a railing that overlooks a long valley, filling already with fall colors, and we're trying to coax him out of the last cave.

"Mom, c'mere!"

"No, *nothing* you say could make me come there this time. We have to *go*." She and I giggle.

"Yeah, Mom, c'mere, look! The mouth of truth!"

We agree that this is probably the *only* thing he could have said, and sure enough, he shows us a stone formation on the wall that looks like a pair of huge lips.

"Why do you call it that?"

He laughs. He has the sweetest disposition imaginable. He had instant, uncritical affection for me when I met him back at the house. "I guess it can't tell lies?"

We head up the last staircase to the parking lot, but he stays back and calls out, "And look. The eyes of wisdom!"

I tell her what a pleasure it is, his endlessly inventive mind, but listening to him has given me a peculiar species of pain— holding out to me, and snatching away from me, *myself*, back when no miser problem kept me from exploring every rocky, mossy detour, and naming the things I found. And he's introducing me to how it will be to play, one day, with my own child. A short walk into the woods, in Martins Creek, and I'd arrive at a small frogpond, clogged with bright green algae. I began visiting it when I was four, did so until age six, when we moved away. I've recently found myself missing this pond more than ever before; I have never loved anything so much as its frogs, tadpoles, turtles, small snakes, salamanders, worms and bugs. Nothing came between us; that mud and bath-warm water seemed to give rise to life itself, and I was its discoverer and first expert. Some days, I'd spend every waking hour stalking specimens, stepping catlike around and around its mucky shore. On May 26, 1966, Mom reports, "When we only had a few minutes before dinner, C. said, 'I think I'll just go out and catch a quick frog.'"

I am thirty-two years old, will soon be thirty-three. At the outset of this Brigid era, I was twenty-four, coiled and set for life to begin. Now here I am again! But whenever I start feeling panicky, self-pitying to have to start all over like this from scratch, hopelessly off-track, I tell myself this story:

"Nine years ago, just before you officially met Brigid, a tall, shiny angel took you by the hand and let you peek at her, this curio, this Muppetty twenty-year-old woman, as she was eating lunch with her friends in the Calhoun College Dining Hall at Yale. See how she amuses everybody, makes them shake their heads and nod their heads, with whatever it is she's telling, with those broad gestures, floppy yet somehow precise, with rapid mouth and that wry compression to her face (she's sending someone up!), then how it suddenly snaps open wide again when she's satisfied at having scored a point. Her hands freeze for a beat or two, cocked as they were when the point was scored. She's in her pea-green corduroy shirt. Across the table, Bernie and Pink are in such breathless pain they're holding on to each other.

"Remember, the angel granted to you full knowledge of her and then said, 'Now, listen carefully, this person is going to die in six years. You may choose to shepherd her along until then, and to *be* shepherded by her. The instant you meet her, you will have to begin adjusting for letting her go. . . . Or else you may bypass her and I will find you someone with whom you can build a long and happy life.'

"At the mention of this second option, you laughed right in the angel's face. *Remember?*"

Lisa grew up a Christian Scientist, used to watch *Mutual of Omaha's Wild Kingdom,* and when Marlin Perkins would transition to a commercial by saying, "Just as the lioness cares for her cubs, so too does Mutual of Omaha care for *you,*" Lisa would see sick people in the commercial being tended at home or in hospital beds. She thought "Mutual of Omaha" must be another name for God, that unseen healing power.

Sonia sat on the back porch, one day when she was a girl, and saw on the cement teeny-tiny red spiders. She shouted into the house, "Mom, what are these red dots?" "They're irritations, honey." For a long time, Sonia thought that's what spiders were called.

The five respondents to my personal ad tell me their childhood misconceptions, and as we talk over dinner, each poor pair of us, I can't help feeling tenderly toward . . . not so much the woman but toward *us,* toward our embarrassed trying. We sip and chew in a low-key fashion, secretly checking the ceiling for the lightning bolt.

At the same time I am smiling at each one of them, though, I can't help, like an ogre, resenting them for treating me like a regular date. Even though it's dimly lit in this restaurant, can't they see the sound of the accident—like winterscene paperweight snow—still hanging in my eyes?

And then there's the miser problem, of course. When I placed the ad, I felt insatiably ready to give myself over to whoever was new, to go on a hundred dates if need be and let them rinse me, burnish me, toss me free of myself. Almost immediately, though, I'm played out, heartsick.

Caroline is sitting on a bench in Northampton when I meet her; I reach down to shake her hand, and she grabs mine with both of hers and pulls me toward her greedily or nervously, so that I have to wrench loose, pretending to be amused. My breathing feels, again, "as thin as a silk thread." I have nothing whatsoever to offer these women beyond certain conversational skills.

They gesture and joke, so optimistically, right here in my face, not up ahead in the ether of the horizon, and I might have known I'd find myself puzzled and annoyed by their particularity (much more than by anything particular *about* them) and by the fact that I'm particular to each of *them*. And make no mistake: The fact of the date itself asks nothing less than that we consider choosing each other, going ahead and letting ourselves be carried off into this exact new world, letting every breath from here on be suffused by this precisely composed atmosphere between us.

Falling in love with a person tells the truth that individuality is the axis of life. Or put it another way—every person is an unduplicated flavor, but it's only when we love her or him that this flavor becomes infinite and we can *taste* it in the world, because the world takes it on and the flavor's source keeps miraculously producing itself, never diluted, day after day after year, even though it has a whole world to fill.

It's an outrage that this person before me—drinking a beer, asking, "So, do you have sisters or brothers?," handling a slice of tomato-and-pesto pizza, getting some on the nail of her baby finger—*presumes* to be that flavor for me. And dreadful vice versa!

Did I feel the outrage back then, at the beginning? If so, it's been swallowed by all that has become, safely, legend.

It's like there's some structure that secretly guides our movement, hallways and then special corners, new angles of light full of surprises. It's like we're both trying but never quite remembering we're trying. We can't seem to see where the corners are. Then there's a moment at which we finally look and say, "Oh, *there* you are."

. . . the image of fates crossing is much too limp for it. It's more like she, or her presence-for-me, is a speedball blistering into my dimension from another, aimed. . . .

I was nibbling at her skin and threatened to eat her up. We had just been talking about freckles—lots, on her arms and even bigger ones on her shoulders and upper back—and she said, "Okay, but leave the freckles, in a little pile on the side."

Before she left, as she was standing at the bottom of the staircase and I was at the top, we went through for each other our favorite ice-cream flavors—butter pecan, mint chocolate chip—as if this were part of an implicit project of settling on a vocabulary for the trivial and day-to-day (but as such the weave of our togetherness), moments and scenes for the future, suddenly becoming encompassed by our zooming-wider horizon.

Often, though, the experience of these dates loses any fine existential dimension, shrinks into self-parody, and I begin to suspect I am silly, just the cartoonishly desperate target of that joke pitch Brigid sent me one day eight months before she died:

MULTINATIONAL LOVE PEBBLES, INC.

162-163 Barre Street, Montpelier, VT 05772

Dear **Miss Noel** ,

Multinational Love Pebbles, Inc. is happy to announce that you are one of the **50** million lucky winners of a hybrid Love Pebble, carefully selected for you based on your personal Love Pebble needs.

When **his** heart is cold as stone, **Miss Noel** , and you feel the need to clench your jaws on something durable and unambiguous, your **Central Vermont** Love Pebble with **Irish** stylings will help you bear the pain of **his** indifference. In your **purse** , tucked away inside your **ear** , or even made into a **delicate jewelry** creation, your individually selected Love Pebble should see you through your darkest hours.

Our Love Pebblists search the world over for both pure-bred and hybrid Pebbles to suit lovers of all ages and types. And the one thing we're sure of after all our research is the overwhelming need out there for Love Pebbles that fit, that are handy and fuel-efficient, that come in a variety of colors and circumferences, suitable for even the most picky **masochist** . In short, **Miss Noel** , we know you're **lonely** sometimes, and **afraid** of what he'll do next, but we know you have what it takes to be strong, and we're proud to have a **little lady** like yourself as a customer.

Remember us. One day, when what's left of your spine has been pounded to a fine powder by this thing you call **love** , and when your **Central Vermont** Love Pebble with **Irish** stylings has long since been **swallowed** or **shattered** , Multinational Love Pebbles, Inc. will be prepared to help you select a new Love Pebble for yourself, and perhaps a stricken friend or family member, too.

We're here for you. And we're going to last.

Yours in support,

Pierre Tantalus

Pierre Tantalus
Executive Vice-Chief President
Multinational Love Pebbles, Inc.
1-800-IAM-ROCK

Have I learned only this, that I am
cleaving to my role in The Story?
The Story, while destroying my
life, has also galvanized it. It is by far the most
profound and fascinating and purifying thing
I've been through, if you include in it meeting
and knowing and loving Brigid all along.

"A few days before the big night," I wrote
in my journal, February 17, 1986,

we looked through her photo album: huge
Irish family: four boys bookended by two girls
—and we talked. I told her about an image
I'd made up—someone wearing something
with sleeves that had "feathers sighing at the
cuffs"—and she said she knew just what I
meant, sort of like how crowds move (this
wasn't what I'd meant, but it was better), how
they'll all be in a big uniform mass, and then
just one or two will move by themselves, sort
of "unpremeditated." I *had* been telling myself to stop funnelling so much significance
into this person whom I wasn't even sure had
the resources to deserve it all, all the sweeping
thoughts about how this could answer my
very secretest needs. But that one word, applied to people's and feathers' movement—
"unpremeditated"—injected me with all the
hope in the world!

The Story does contain a desire for its own ending, but I see now that that desire is, perhaps, only an idea, and there are two kinds of ideas, those that want to remain ideas and those that want to pass as soon as possible into substance. We can hop back to C. S. Lewis for a moment, to where in *Surprised by Joy* he describes the peculiarly open-ended quality of true joy as "that of an unsatisfied desire which is itself more desirable than any other satisfaction."

In other words, this particular Story is much too good to put down; I'm still engrossed.

If I were to step outside it, out of center stage where the spotlight tilts onto me luridly, I'm afraid I would find myself out of the theater altogether, landed in the parking lot, in the quotidian light of an ordinary afternoon. My difficulties would not, then, be different in kind from any average person's! Can you imagine *me*, an average person? Just as though nothing much had happened? Never!

No, I'm tucked, cloaked in my identity as Tragedy Victim, and it has served me well. I have never been more famous, to *myself*.

If the shoe were on the other foot, I'll bet Brigid would be loving the me that is me rather than the me that is my impact upon her. But still, for some reason, since I cannot marry her, I seem to be choosing to marry my Epic Emptiness and Pain, and these are made even more ghostly—more like Brigid now?—by my shocking lust for them.

Yes, I love it up here alone in my little office room, typing away, sucking down red wine, eating spaghetti topped with tomato sauce and hot Italian sausages that are bad for me. I let out a laugh like a vampire and go on sucking my own blood. Outside my window, drizzle seethes on School Street.

Sunday. I arrive at the Unitarian Universalist church, a five-minute walk from my house, for the third Sunday in a row, and I'm in a snarly, impatient mood. The choir takes the stage and gets going on a Scottish folk tune. There are a couple of old people, singing merrily (an old woman bobs from side to side with a giant smile), a young, very fat man, a sad-seeming misfit, then middle-aged women and men, each with very particular faces, some on the radiant side, some quite wooden.

It's just the sort of scene you'd find in a movie, or read about in a novel—the good souls, up there, holding forth, making a sonorous tableau, a performative pause in the ongoing sweep of life. In the movie or the novel, we love them inordinately for representing to us our own capacity to take time out, love them for enacting the simple celebratory principle. There's often a voice-over that comes in to eclipse the singers' voices, though not their faces, and to explain how life went on after this day.

In *Our Town,* Dr. Ferguson's choir has continuing trouble with a drunken organist, a man who tries to find peace and transcendence but ends up killing himself. The choir's presence in that play, as I recall, connects with the whole feeling of the stately march of the town through time, the conscientious gathering for worship and consecration in the church where George and Emily get married, where Emily's funeral is held soon thereafter.

I've never been more moved by any scene than I was when I

first read *Our Town* in high school, when Emily was granted permission to return to the world just once, and she chose her twelfth birthday. Of course she cannot bear to remain more than a few minutes: her family can't see her and answer what she says to them; she knows what's going to happen in the future, and her parents and little brother (later to die of a burst appendix) do not; and finally, it's all too hideously, piercingly beautiful, as the living hardly notice. Emily says good-bye to things—Good-bye, coffee . . . good-bye, clocks ticking, et cetera—and then to the Stage Manager she says, "Oh, earth, you're too wonderful for anybody to realize you. Do any human beings ever realize life *while* they live it?—every, every minute?" And he answers, "No. The saints and poets, maybe—they do some."

At the time, at age seventeen, I told myself, Oh, *I will* realize it.

But funny thing: Now I myself have moved through an Emily-like vision of radiance passing into dark, and rather than carpeing any diem, I've gone, with her, the other way, back up the hill to the graveyard, to sit on and on patiently, getting "weaned away from earth."

Everything seems lacquered over with gray. Sometimes, I force myself out of this apartment and have "fun"; but it only seems to splash off me like water off a hunk of clay. Beautiful days I resent and feel either oppressed by or just dimly distant from. These fall colors look like flat photographs to me. Actually, that's how all the seasons seem—backdrop pictures and a wind machine. This one's certainly better than spring, when everything *else* is coming back to life; I'm actually looking forward to the deathly charcoals of November.

I can't help it. This choir seems dopey, and the hundred worshipers deadly dull, even though what brings them all here can't be dull, can it? Y' know, the flame that burns steadily within each of us.

A woman climbs the stairs onto the stage and takes her spot at the pulpit. Jeanne Kocsis is reporting on her recent trip to Transylvania, now part of Romania, where "we" have a sister church in a village of five hundred called Homorodkaracsony-falva.

I look up at one of the carefully soft-core-spiritual stained-glass windows (tapioca sky, jade-green hills), at the bottom of which are the words "with the morn/come angels' smiles/we have lost awhile." I'm not irredeemably misanthropic, I believe. I know I could open myself to any one of these people, because of course each is an angel in her or his own right, but here I am stuck in the notion that my "morn" can only be truly heralded by a fascinating young woman.

Even before the accident, and even though Brigid voiced deep-running ambivalence about marriage and children, I felt I was crossing with her a suspension bridge between the solid rock of my original family and that of the family we'd eventually make together. Now I'm still on a bridge between families, but it's become a very rickety, viny, South American sort, blowing in the wind. The easy response to this image is that I mustn't seek salvation and solidity outside myself. But why not? Most of what I understand about solidity bursts right out of that first snowball on black bark, and my mother hovering above my shoulder. I want to hover above a shoulder. My mother gave me the world and the means to love it. Giving the same, I'll return it to myself, in the circling style of such things. " 'She gave me love,' writes Toby Talbot of her mother, 'to love myself, and to love the world. I must remember how to love.' "

Swing on this bridge, hold on tight and try to find my steps —I am not based or girded enough yet to love the world or its people. At least this is how I assuage my guilt about always squandering the endless miracles, the angels' smiles, all around me, holding my breath and withholding my vision (making people into cardboard cutouts), hoping in every next woman I meet to find the gateway to Three-Dimensional Real Life.

Real life in Homorodkaracsonyfalva, it turns out, grinds on day by day in crushing poverty. Jeanne Kocsis tells us from the pulpit that most of the people she met there are very pale and thin and either don't own/have access to land or are too weak to farm it. Only 20 percent of the arable land in town is used to grow food. This is partly because of the malnutrition—which certainly doesn't breed industriousness—and partly because of a scarcity of tractors.

Jeanne Kocsis arrived in Homorodkaracsonyfalva secretly carrying thirty-three hundred-dollar bills in a money belt. Under Ceauşescu, all contact with the outside world had been forbidden. Now suddenly there was a group from America who cared about their welfare and stood eager to exchange goodwill and information, and even to hand them tractor money. She and the minister had an adventure in the black market before securing enough Romanian currency to purchase a plain, used, but functional, bright orange tractor. It took all day for them to get it back to the village, and then at the Sunday service the people sniffled and cried and prayed to be worthy of this gift. Every single member of the congregation brought her a bouquet of flowers, and she asks us, today, in closing, who has received the greater gift, we or they?

I cry too, of course, sitting here: I am human, it's good to be reminded. Jeanne Kocsis has become, sure enough, through her talk, warm and three-dimensional, someone I'd love to eat a chicken dinner with. I am sorry I felt so heartless toward her as toward them all; just to look at her, you'd never suspect she recently held an armload of flowers in a cold, hungry village. Isn't my frigidity made of the same stuff as the wind that blows across Homorodkaracsonyfalva? Oh, I claim to be more village than wind. But they embraced our envoy *before* she bought them the tractor, whereas I want the tractor *first.* And probably I wouldn't even *accept* an old, no-frills, bright orange one! I'd probably hold out for teal, a heated cab with a music system. I might demand to be taken to tractor expos, walk up and down the aisles, rubbing my chin. "Hmmm, no, I don't think so, not *feisty* enough . . . not wise and playful enough, as tractors go . . . uh-uh, certainly sexy but not . . . y' know, *surreptitiously* sexy. No, no, no, no, no."

three

Octtober 2. Twenty months now. I'm driving along Route 9 northeast of town, my window wide open, breathing inside a stream of surprisingly warm, humid air. And suddenly— "What's that?"—there is something strange in the atmosphere, both unmistakable and mysterious.

It has been a good day. This afternoon, I had a captivating two-and-a-half-hour lunch with, yes, a *woman* whom I'd met before and who just happened through town today. She is a fiction writer, about twenty-five, with *both* a sharp wit and heart-cupping brown eyes. What more could I ever want?

Over ice cream cones, she told me about an adventure she had as a teenager, scuba diving, about forty feet down, off the coast of Australia. She came upon a convention of manta rays, dozens, lying flat on the sand all around her, shimmying their wings to stir up the water, which helps them to breathe.

She and I shimmied our wings at each other too, flirting, and I decided then and there to go ahead and take up scuba diving myself, a plot I've long had at the back of my mind.

The next day, I thumb through the yellow pages and call an outfit that just happens to be starting a scuba course; several days later, I'm in a classroom and in a swimming pool with four other men and an instructor who's a former marine and acts like it, though he has a heart. Eleven days later, after learning all about the equipment and various diving conditions and nitrogen toxicity and the effects of pressure on the human body, and after passing all the written and swimming-pool performance tests—except the endurance swimming exam; I never even learned the crawl as a kid, but my instructor finally lets this slide—I'm in wet suit and full gear twenty-five feet beneath the surface of the ocean, off Cape Ann, Massachusetts, holding a small skate—part of the ray family—by the tail and watching him flap.

I smooth-kick my flippers and glide past four-foot "striper" fish and over rocks and crevasses, into which crabs and lobsters rush away as I chase them with my hands. I try to breathe slow, slow, pulling long, industrial-sounding breaths into my poor alien lungs. Down here, you must try to relax into a fluid environment, as in space. You are "neutrally buoyant," weightless, so that even the solid ocean floor provides no solidity. You are breathing precious air through the plastic regulator clenched between your teeth, exhaling bubbles that travel back up to your own atmosphere, which holds itself steady above you as a backlit sheet but to which you cannot return more quickly than one foot per second, even in an emergency, on pain of death. Stay calm!—even though you are blatantly on the verge, each moment, of catastrophe. Rising too fast, even from ten feet down, can bring "the bends," bubbles of nitrogen forming in the bloodstream, traveling to the brain, causing a potentially fatal embolism.

"What's that?" It finally hits me as I approach Northampton that what's up isn't anything new in the weather but rather in me. My breathing feels *round*, not flat, for the first time in these twenty months. I haven't even been aware it *was* flat, but right now it is suddenly an entirely different activity from what I've been engaged in.

(My father didn't get glasses until he was eight years old, and only then did he realize that one was *supposed* to see individual leaves on the trees rather than hazy patches of green.)

My lungs have unfurled like spring leaves, or like crumpled sponges dropped into water, and each breath is lavish, an un-sleepy yawn that says, "You are just where you should be and the story of your life is back on track!" The air stirs around in me, broadly, puffing into vapor the rotten cabbage in my chest. I can tell now that I have been, more than metaphorically, an organism long in contraction.

Later that night, though, the roundness diminishes, the cabbage reclaims its home, and by the next day—by the time I open the yellow pages—I am breathing flat again, this time knowing it.

And now that I've learned to dive, it's come clear that everyday breathing is, for me, like breathing from a tank underwater. Not that I can't inhale and exhale deeply, but deep or shallow, it's the same story: arrow in, arrow out. Utilitarian, introducing the necessary oxygen into my system to avoid crisis. It's an urgency born of scarcity, a clunky procedure allowing for survival in a foreign, always implicitly hostile environment.

In the diving class, we were taught a miraculous truth about gases under pressure. At a depth of thirty-three feet, a chestful of compressed air actually contains twice as many molecules as a chestful at the surface; at sixty-six feet, three times as many, and so on. Which means that as you rise, the pressure on your lungs (which has packed the extra air in) is relieved, and the air expands. Another danger of too-rapid ascent, therefore, is ruptured lungs.

But the compensatory blessing of this expansion is that if your breathing tube or regulator (mouthpiece) breaks, and if you can keep your head and come up slowly, under control, you can make it to the surface easily from *any* depth, there being plenty of oxygen already in your lungs. This is called a free ascent.

Our instructor showed us how, sat us on the ocean floor and removed our regulators. As I rose gradually, twenty feet, I felt air breeding within my lungs, forcing itself out my throat; I wasn't short of breath at all.

The day before, Dennis Clark, Brigid's father, had died of kidney failure brought about by prostate cancer.

When I first met him, he hid behind a tree and jumped out at me, wearing his black-and-gold Ohio State jacket. Under water, I remember how upset Brigid was by his cancer and his grim prognosis—"one to three years." She couldn't get him to talk seriously about dying; the Clarks, except her, never relished full frontal emotion—he'd make dark jokes or, at most, reiterate his wish that his wake be a blowout Irish dance party. He almost made it the three years.

As I held the skate off Cape Ann, watched it flap then let it go, I hoped Brigid was less anxious now. She has her father's mouth. The skate disappeared into the cold gloom that surrounded our diving group, and we swam on.

*first
hypnosis
session,
october 27,
9:00 a.m.*

"Open your hand on your lap," says my therapist, in her soft voice, "and hold the fingers out straight. Look at them. You'll begin to notice slight movements in these fingers, and these movements will become clearer and clearer. That's happening now. And eventually, your hand will begin to rise, of its own accord, toward your face. That's beginning to happen too."

Well, maybe a tiny bit, but it's weighted by my awareness that I am being plied by such a standard routine, my fear that I will not be hypnotizable, and even by my ambivalence about the project itself: to try to reapproach Brigid, after this long, gray detour, to spend time together with her again, at most to relive experiences or have new conversations, or at least to encounter her in that crisp, immediate way C. S. Lewis promised, rather than let her remain contained, near but safe, undisturbed and undemanding, in the Castle Keep.

"Now turn your hand back over and rest it in your lap. Close your eyes, and picture yourself at the top of a long, carpeted staircase. You have bare feet and the carpet feels good under them. You can look down the staircase as it curves off to the left, and you can see it has twenty steps and its carpet gets thicker and deeper-colored the farther down it goes. What color is that carpet?"

"Um, I guess dark green."

"That's right, it *is* dark green."

"How the hell do you know? You're wrong, okay, it's *red!*" But I don't say this, I make a good-faith effort to place myself into this reality, and I notice, to my relief, that I am able to envision *some* of this, though only in patches, and that though my head feels trapped in a bubble of cynicism, my body feels like a tuning fork that has been lightly struck—there is a definite vibration through me, not fading, comforting. Noticing this heartens me, lets me answer "two" when asked how deep in trance I feel, from zero to ten.

But I never stop hearing the cars going by outside on the street, extra loud because it's been raining, and I never really get deeper, don't make it far down the dark green stairs, much less into the safe room at the bottom, so she tries another tack.

"Now you're sitting in a theater, in a very soft chair. You're very comfortable and are looking up to the stage, where a curtain is about to open. When it does, you will see that a play is under way, a play about you and your current situation in life."

Well, the curtain opens, and in a funny way—half forced and half spontaneous—I *do* see some things. A vague me-figure is at center stage, and all around, close to him but not close enough to touch, are many women, each in a different state of defectiveness. They aren't recognizable as individuals, but one has an extralong, gangly arm, and another has a slice taken out of her head. None of the others is even that clear, but I know they are all handicapped and kind of dancing, herky-jerky, taunting. And behind it all, there is a huge white backdrop, with Brigid's gigantic shadow, mostly just her head, in profile, motionless, reminding me of a puppet just hanging on a wall, unused.

Afterward, while driving to Bread & Circus for the healthful salad I ritually buy and eat after therapy, I keep seeing this shadow again and again, until it finally starts dancing too, in that manic, floppy way Brigid had, and now it's her whole upper body, still mostly in profile, but abandoned and joyful, arms flapping around wildly, like when she'd be pretending to throw a fit. I start to cry and have to wait in the Bread & Circus parking lot for a while until I can go inside.

The twenty-one-month mark has come and gone. Milestones are passing like phone poles on the road; I can't grab them.

It's a warm Indian summer afternoon, and I'm jogging my two-mile dirt-road loop through tall cornstalks. A light thunderstorm is coming.

My friend Joy and I have just this week started sleeping together. She's been my mainstay, has grieved with me. She is a brilliant fiction writer and says things that dump buckets of confectioners' sugar onto my heart. She's like Brigid (and me, *and* that boy Nicholas) in that she comes up with little notions, plays with silly concepts that would miss most people by a mile but that strike me right through the core. Like this: "What if it were so dark you couldn't see your own neck?" Or: "Just try to *imagine* the difference between Dopey and Sneezy." We find it darling, the way the mind struggles in vain to wrap itself around such proposals. "Could this be a successful advertising slogan: 'It's the *kind* of food you'll *laugh about!*'" "What do you think would be the shortest amount of time it would take, once you'd had a baby, before you could get twenty dollars from it?"

And she's convulsed by mine: "What if you loved someone so much your hand shrank to keep pace with his balding, so that he could feel your hand enjoying a steady degree of luxury and lostness in his remaining hair?"

We can go on and on, even when we wake up at 5:00 A.M. That's, for me, a major romantic criterion, that the person and I take each other for fanciful rides, that we be able to laugh ourselves sick before sunrise.

Add to this quirky intersection the fact that we're hugely attracted to each other and have wonderful sex.

I've been going on the assumption that to attain perfect solitude, the purity of an empty vessel, will best ready me for refilling with Brigid's presence. But this posture, poised for reapproach, has gotten me nowhere. The Polo Ball experience crystallized the precious pathos of my aloneness, handed it back to me so I could hug it. By being a genuine and complicated Other, Joy questions it, disrupts it, lets earth outweigh transcendence, gives me back the texture of my embodiment as a person not ethereal, not "too beautiful for the world," but scared-happy-sick-impressive-weak. And maybe it's this that can leave me open to reapproach in unexpected ways. Quit hanging in ether! Dive back into the mud and rock and roots and tangle, because Brigid's here too, and possibly closer by.

Every now and then, I stop running and walk, feel the rain and wind on my skin and try hard to feel, as well, whether Brigid might not be here with me in a whole different way from the flamboyant embrace other mourners report. I am cheered by

Emily Dickinson's idea that "Minds in the same ground meet by tunnelling." Is it some "disarmingly simple" proximity that I have numbed myself to in prepping for a grand Second Coming? But how to know it? Feeling rain and wind on my skin is a storm-walking cliché; but "feeling" Brigid in me nonvisibly, nonaudibly, even nonsensuously . . . that's so far from a cliché that a whole new language will be needed, one that can match, nuance for nuance, the small movements of someone who is kept in a black sack inside a black chamber. Or am I only kidding myself with all this semantic crap, ennobling what is, in me, an essential lameness of spirit? I could learn to live with either, but what if the two are forever indistinguishable?

Why it's not perfect with Joy—besides that I want marriage and children and she shudders at the former and finds the latter irresponsible in light of world population growth—is that we also distinctly diverge in temperament, me quite even-keeled and (maybe too) rational, cringing at sudden flares of temper, even if they're justified. Joy hates it when I cringe at hers. And I'm almost always (maybe too) evenhanded, ready to give the other side the benefit of the doubt, seeing gray where she tends to see black and white.

But nobody keeps me better company. When we're not fighting, exercising a hideous leverage upon each other, I crave nothing in this town (besides being alone) but to spend time with Joy, cooking dinners, reading aloud, going for walks.

Appreciating me elaborately, she makes me a more dimensionally living creature right here and now and, in this, leaves me weaker too, though not in the way that Polo Ball did. This isn't a thinning down to a silk thread, to lights-out invisibility.

I pick up the pace as the storm rises; thunder rattles my knees. What if no vision or visitation is coming my way, and I will simply never, even in dreams, spend any more time with her?

Shoe on the other foot, Brigid would be communing with me much more heroically, I know it! Her brokenness would be shocking to behold and my soul would gather like these clouds overhead. Images of me would burst down on her night and day.

I'll never forget the sounds that came out of her the night she found our dog Pearl—a nine-month-old sheltie, Romeo's predecessor—hit and dead on the side of the road, a dusting of snow over her brown and white fur. I was way off across the field, searching, calling "Pearlie!" in case she'd wandered into the woods (though in actuality afraid to look at the road), when Brigid, scanning the edges of Route 14 with a flashlight, let out a series of high screams that kept coming as I ran across the half-frozen mud. I hated knowing her lungs could slam out into the night like this, and how every next scream had to rudely rush the one before, like waves thrown by something offshore, something huge and nearing so that the waves got taller and faster. She sobbed in bed for nights, and I was the composed one holding her. For months she'd remind me of little things Pearl would do, like sneak up behind our legs if we were standing at the kitchen counter and poke her needly snout between our knees, whereupon we'd squeeze it. And a lot of other things I'd forgotten, things I can't remember now, again. Effortlessly, she held her whole. She showed me how to mourn that dog.

You are in a comfortable chair in front of a television set. With this remote, you can switch the channels and turn the volume up and down to adjust the emotional intensity of what you're viewing." She says I'm watching a program that has information in it that I especially need.

I wish.

But then I start to get some reception. I'm two-thirds thinking it and only one-third actually seeing it, but it's a sort of show about me in all my efforts. There's me at my desk pecking away at this writing. There's me lying on the therapy couch. In flashes, I'm at the desk and on the couch *outdoors,* in a field, and I realize that in trying to pursue my truth so industriously, in focusing so sternly, I'm unable to experience the "outdoors" itself, a certain wind that must be blowing. I wish I could be like a sail, filling, or like a tree, or something very porous that could feel the wind rushing through.

Shortly after the accident, I started telling people that Brigid seemed to me to have been an event in nature, one that I was lucky enough to have witnessed.

Then her dying literally took her into the pure "nature" part of herself, you could say, and certainly also the suddenness, the sheer Occurrence Quality of the accident, stripped of thinking or thinkability, is like the world-without-minds.

Our good friend Heidi went to see Brigid at the funeral home on the day in between the accident and the memorial service. She hasn't told me about this visit yet, because I haven't felt ready to hear it. She has said that it wasn't scary because Brigid was "not there."

A poem written by Stan Rice, after the death of his six-year-old daughter, concludes: "look! a shaft of light pierces the dust-ball: just that effortlessly/she went."

None of this busy endeavoring to "come to terms" has been conducted in nature's own terms, whatever they may be. I guess my staring into space comes the closest, because it doesn't try anything, lets go, like Keats's negative capability, of any "irritable reaching after fact and reason."

All of a sudden I am deeper in trance without thinking myself there, without any gimmicks. The therapist is trying to get me to go back in time five years. Brigid and I would have been living at the top of East State Street in Montpelier. But I'm fuzzy—I am refusing to go where she's asking me to.

Instead, I am going nowhere, have no images, not even ones invented dutifully by my brain, eager to please. I'm just falling into heaviness, a kind that's wholly undreamed of. The therapist's voice is alarmingly far away, sounding like that of an ant over on a hilltop. I am collapsing into density, overwhelming, stonelike density, collapsing fast, and I'm a little frightened. I tell her, and she says I have ultimate control over my state. My hands are really heavy, folded on my belly, not at all sentient, as when you've been sleeping on an arm and wake up to find it just as good as dead. But these hands are not pressing down on my belly particularly, because my belly too, my whole torso, is made out of rock. I get flickers of the windy field again, and I'm now a mossy boulder, half sunk in earth, at the border between woods and field. I'm folding away from all language and perception, and I can be gigantic because I'm everything, there's no "outside" to measure myself against. It feels as if all my staring into space and rotting has aspired to exactly this, getting out past the brink, finding density without rescue. But instead of "finding," as an act, it's as though relaxing has brought this on, as though this density has found *me*, as though, throughout these twenty-one months, I have after all only been secretly fighting it off.

The therapist is saying, "Allow yourself to feel everything you feel," but the truth is I feel absolutely nothing but my billion pounds, although of course, in my head, there's still the good-soldier tinny version of emotion marching around, trying to follow orders.

It seems it would not take much to snip the thread that still ties me to the antlike voice, and then like a dying star from which (so they say) even light cannot escape, I would finally tumble effortlessly all the way down, so that even theories, metaphors, plans could not escape. Then I could be, and the wind could blow and anything could happen and I wouldn't care.

But even short of that entirety, even as I am now, Brigid

herself could not be less relevant. I am supposed to be moving toward her, but I'm only losing her the more thoroughly.

When I'm awake again, sitting up and returned to one hundred and eighty pounds, the therapist suggests I ponder what I've been through, and it occurs to me that that word is related to *ponderous*. (Language-Boy, reporting for duty again!) At home, the dictionary gives "ponder" as "to weigh," and I see it can be both transitive and intransitive. Have I been too much on the transitive side, missing out on what I myself weigh? And what would that mean?

Back in January, for the first anniversary of Brigid's accident, I wrote six pages, my first try at getting any of this down. At one point, I quoted from Brigid's journal, right at the end, where she lists the ten scariest things. The top three are "(1) Being murdered; (2) Killing someone by accident—car; (3) Dying in an accident: fire, drowning, crash."

The last three words of her journal, before page after page of blank, are "Taking myself seriously."

"I dutifully write your words down," I said beneath those excerpts, "getting them right. What kind of task is that, what duty? Taking full measure of your crushing, pressing your frustration to a radiant limit? . . . I think I must wish to make you a poor poor horrible monster, bellowing Medusa, to turn us all to stone, to the relief of stone at last."

Thanksgiving. Visiting Vermont, our old house, I am helping two men budge our woodstove—as heavy as I was under hypnosis!—out the door. I've sold it for six hundred dollars, this jade-colored Hearthstone soapstone we felt so lucky to inherit from the previous owners. I thought this might be my last chance, since HUD is about to foreclose on me, lock me out, because my tenants have gone and I've stopped paying the mortgage, because I didn't want to dump into this chasm the last of my share of the money Mr. and Mrs. Clark were awarded in the lawsuit against the woman who hit Brigid. I won't give the government that money; I'm going to find some better way to spend it.

The man who bought the stove wanted it as a Christmas present for his mother. He and his brother and I take frequent rests; it has taken twenty minutes to go twenty feet, but we make it onto the front porch and, triumphantly, into the back of a pickup.

I sit in my car and watch the stove shrinking away through my side mirror, and only then do I get any film: Brigid shoving logs in through its swung-open side door; her working the bellows, frustrated at the recalcitrance of the fire; her adding water to the cast-iron dragon her sister, Conna, gave her the last Christmas (it sits on top and spews steam out its nose!); thick, sixteen-inch pieces of wood filling her arms (three or four are all she can manage, bark and chips and mud get on the front and sleeves of the drab green coat she always throws on before going into the icy cellar where the wood's stacked); the horrible crashing sound when these heavy logs hit the big, round steel basin next to the stove (it always seems to me she drops them from too great a height, rather than bending to set or at least roll them in); and there, she's kneeling to open the side door, rummaging around inside the fire with the long metal poker, flinching and withholding her face because of the heat.

When the pickup has disappeared, I get out of the car and sneak back inside. That stove kept us warm for two winters and was the hovering point for all visitors, and for us. Without it, this house is even more a vacant husk.

There's no electricity now; all the pipes have frozen solid because I missed the chance to drain them and have the city shut my water off. There is filthy, puffy, gray-pink insulation spilled in heaps on the floor by inspectors hired by a prospective buyer whose financing has suddenly fallen through; and these inspectors have also strewn a fine yellow dust all over the main downstairs floor. I try to jolly myself by quipping silently that this dust is like pollen left by a bee the size of a cow. The air in here is absolutely dim and frigid. Strips of plaster hang from the ceiling in the living room, which reminds me that two independent inspectors so far have determined that part of our foundation is crumbling away. The whole house, around me, seems the definition of dull, null matter. Out back, some neighbor boys have built the ugliest tree house in the world from green-painted and bare plywood, sheets of dirty plastic. I climb upstairs to find that my ladder, borrowed by an inspector, still sticks up through the opened hatch in the ceiling, into the two-foot-high crawl space beneath the flat roof. Relax, I tell myself, there is no heat to escape!

I've tried to learn to throw up my hands. It's something that doesn't come naturally to me. I mean, it's easy to throw them up in the face of a given frustration, but in *general*, the *whole things?* I always seem to hold back, to save a solid, imaginary copy of my hands, which I keep *down*.

I don't walk down into the basement now and smash empty jars and bottles on the concrete floor, in the corner, although I did this a few times last year. And I don't walk into the bedroom and lie down on the blank floor, as near as I can estimate to the spot I occupied—two feet higher—in bed the morning she left, don't look up at where she stood and try to bring her in, and I don't get up and stand exactly where she stood, seeing myself lying below just trying to get back to sleep, although I did this once, a couple months ago.

I don't spend much time here at all today; I've only returned to retrieve a pair of work gloves. Wouldn't you think this inert building would suit me well, answer to the stone I now recognize as myself? But standing here within the howling emptiness of this house, I feel, again, the rare sensation: low in my belly, lava, like a secret lake of it bubbling and starting to rise. Not only a stone after all, I feel like if this lava keeps rising, I will begin to tear this house down!

But as always over these past months, as quickly as it rises, it recedes, till it's just far and feathery, like a memory of sex.

Back in the car, shifting into third, I fantasize about burning the house down or blowing it up. The idea calls the lava again, and I feel the glimmerings of a tremendous pent heat, actually frightening. On second thought, fire or a bomb is too quick and easy. What I really want is to be in a ferocious physical battle for my life.

Perfect would be: I am lowered onto a small island on which lives a beast, a beast who happens to be *furious* at me!

I know this is silly, sitting now in this comfy desk chair and fancying such a matchup, yet astonishingly, even writing the word *furious* starts the lava rising just a shade. It *wants* to rise, is hunting a way up. Sitting quietly, tickled by this curious enormity, sedate, reasonable, evenhanded, I know nevertheless that if this substance were to climb through my belly, I'd darn well have to stop typing; when it reached my chest I'd explode, ecstatic—but where to?

I could track down and torture the woman who killed Brigid, but this thought immediately diminishes the lava—must be I am not angry at her. Or is it that striking at her is too neat and tidy, logical? I want to destroy without reason, outrageously, as indifferent to my targets as nature was twenty-two months ago, in the form of an ice patch.

Once, a short while after the accident, I dreamed that Brigid and I were having a normal day, except that the doctor had told us she would soon succumb to something called hurricane pneumonia. We found it odd that this could be anticipated but not avoidable, and that she could feel fine today. We were only, though, *mildly* alarmed; it didn't seem credible.

I wish I could take on the hurricane, in both senses of "take on." Not so mild anymore, I'd be trafficking, finally, *in it,* feeling the brunt of a far catastrophe that still seems closer to hearsay than to fury.

Is this recent urge to destroy the leading edge of the storm finally reaching me? I used to think that if I could really meet it, I might find Brigid somehow tucked behind its teeth, like finding Hope left at the bottom of Pandora's box.

One way to respond to a storm when it overtakes you is, of course, to get the feeling you *are* that storm, to take on its full identity—spitting lightning, coughing up wind, producing thunder from your heart. If I could do violence myself, real violence, not caring for consequences, just *lashing!* what occurred would stop being the filmy, old unthinkable thought, would rip itself right up through me like new, like clean, white voltage.

But it's hard to get there, because what I'm closest to being furious at is not Brigid or the other woman but elusiveness, the elusiveness of what emerged, what smashed her in the head and the spleen and the leg, and then disappeared again. I know it's a mystification to think of it as a particular something that can be flushed and held. But the way it moved, that's what I come to.

I said that I wanted to take on the storm in both senses. Doing storm-work is taking it on as one takes on a task. How about driving to Tennessee, say, randomly picking a small town, and with a machete hacking everything and everyone in it to bloody, sizzling bits, including pets, including the goldfish, mincing them?

But on the other side, I want to take on the storm as an adversary, take up *for* Brigid herself, small and marked, take her part.

One night, in 1987, she sat up in bed and shouted, "Is the monster here yet?"

"No, not yet," I said, and she lay back down.

We laughed about that ever after.

Yes, lower me onto the island where the beast lives.

Oh, listen to him, my God—he is so angry with me he can't contain it! He's practically choking on it! For the first whole day and night, I sit still, here on a rock high on the beach, and hear him screaming, in the thick forest at the center of the island. I have no idea what he will look like, but he won't look that way for long once I get a crack at him. He is beside himself with rage, breaking his throat, but he has absolutely no reason to hate me; he's never even met me.

I'm not standing up and running toward him, because I'm only sitting in my desk chair. My lava hovers, hoping this fantasy will deepen and get more vivid. I wish I could really dream my way onto that terrible island. I can hardly wait to lay my hands on the bloodthirsty thing, because if I'm laying my hands on him, that will mean he's finally *here*.

December 1, and it hits me.

I *will* go after the beast.

I drive for four hours through the muted, lightly singed countryside, between fall and winter, and though the lava still refuses to rise past its certain modest level beneath my navel, a hunger rises, a hunger for the *literal* confrontation with wildness, for something that will answer my wish, will be truly large and worthy of pushing against with all this mounting pressure in me.

Scuba diving certification card firmly in pocket, I picture the vast and powerful world under a tropical sea; and then I picture a deep green, steamy jungle.

With shocking definitiveness, I drive back to Northampton and waltz into the immaculate office of a travel agent, receive brochures, crystallize plans. In February, I will fly to Belize for eleven days; I will dive under the sea and I will trek into the rain forest. It's expensive, but I will spend the lawsuit money on *this*!

No, it's not likely I'll find my monster wrapped neatly inside a package deal from the fine folks at "Travel Belize, Ltd., of Boulder, Colorado." But that country is apparently still relatively uncommodified, and, after all, the jungle is the jungle, the ocean is the ocean, and who knows what they have to ante up versus my gambit? At least there are any number of genuine dangers for me to envision in these places. Maybe one of them will suddenly flash out, furious at me for no good reason.

Since I now know how suited I am to my Story, how infatuated with it, why not try to write it even bolder—"Boulder" is a sign!—in order to step it up, to press it to a limit?

I have learned something new. Off the coast of Belize there is a formation which, from the air, appears to be a nearly circular crater or basin in the sea, ringed by coral reefs and filled with very dark blue water. Jacques Cousteau took his *Calypso* and crew on expedition there in 1972, dove inside—despite legends of sea monsters residing there—and found that it opens out beneath the surface into a cavern, complete with stalactites and tunnels moving off from the main chamber. This system seems to have developed above sea level, before the melting of the last Ice Age caused the water to rise, filling the cavern in and weakening its ceiling until it collapsed and left the opening we see today.

Measuring 1,045 feet across, its coral rim stands in just fifteen feet of water. Cousteau's minisub sonar revealed that this main chamber reaches a depth of nearly 500 feet.

I have learned that a few companies run trips out to the Blue Hole—three hours off-shore—and take parties of advanced divers down. Maybe I could *tell* them I'm advanced, not say I've only ever poked around in a protected bay north of Boston.

December 30, 1965: Before he went to bed C. said he wanted to say a prayer so he folded his hands, we had to close eyes, and he said, "O God, please keep me safe forever. Amen."

Dear Brig,

Obviously, it's really scary and somehow very hard for me to do this and feel like I'm actually talking to you rather than just performing, which would be a good argument for not trying it within the public/private confines of this memoir, but which is also why I'm able to . . . the Castle Keep, insulation, I don't know, maybe a witness (the reader) for moral support. How can I be afraid of you?

Plus, I'm not sure if you just know everything now, making a letter superfluous.

I find myself already reading this over and thinking of revision-ideas, which shows I'm not feeling connected enough.

Anyway, the other day, in therapy, I started feeling a way that I could only describe as sour, and the therapist said it made her think of sour milk, and I said soured by the vinegar of self-consciousness, of grief orchestration. Later, playing basketball at the Y, I realized I felt smutty. I thought, It's Christmas, for God's sake, where's my fucking generosity, why have I shuffled Brigid herself right out of the picture? Even in saying that, I put you in the third person instinctively! I wanted to give you a present. I started thinking about your being alive and my being dead and your deciding to get me something anyway, but I didn't get very far because my imagination balked as it always does when I try to really go somewhere with it about or toward you. I've often gotten comfort, though, from supposing us in the opposite shoes, even though I'm only able to bring in glimpses of your life—as much as a quick snapshot of you, sitting, devastated, being ministered to by our friends and our family . . . it makes me feel tremendously better for a moment, like we've got a job to do together, a division of labor. We're doing well, acquitting ourselves admirably, and would be able to go back and exchange responsibilities, spell each other.

But one reason I feel like you'd be purer in missing me is that you've always been better at it, this long-distance relating. As you remember, I am usually quite good at being with a person when I'm with them, but more shaky at being with them when I'm not. You have both gifts, I guess just the second one now, the one I could use. It feels good writing directly to you—better than avoiding it, at least—but I still don't feel successfully in touch. I feel guilty that your letters to me were always so thorough, wonderfully obsessively expansive, whereas mine were much measlier, and now not only do I not read your letters over but it has taken owing you a letter for almost two years for me finally to get around to writing you! If only I knew you were on the other end, all else, all distracting veils, would peel away and I swear I would write you two hundred pages before Christmas. I actually think I can really swear this! Especially if I also knew you needed me to tell you things, if otherwise you were cut off and just wondering, wondering. You would be so filled up with news, I would write and write, even if you couldn't reply even a little. Of course I would ask you a million questions anyway, just knowing you could understand them. It would be the greatest experience of my life. There is so ridiculously much to tell. Maybe after two hundred pages my miserdom would have a good bite taken out of it!

Those lines from your good old story "Snow" keep coming back, now printed neatly on page 63 of the book your mom and dad made for you (Hey! How is it having him there??? Just comforting, or do you still feel he only partially knows you???): "The Himalayas are howling tonight: something must be amiss. Are you there? I seem to feel you knocking on my chest, dissatisfied. I am a sad bone, sometimes in your clutching hand, sometimes safe between the teeth of the sage."

Naturally I hear this now in Heidi's voice—at your memorial reading two Mays ago—rather than in yours, even though I remember crying at your first MFA reading, at how moved by and inside your story you were, how you were always on the verge of crying. God, you were so radiantly talented, your voice so authoritative that night. I was so proud of you.

But you know all this. Is it good to be reminded, or doesn't that make any sense anymore? These questions are hatefully abstract.

Among the violences all of this perpetrates is a violence to the shape of time.

You weren't dead and we were in the present, like a spearhead or the prow of a ship, all the past spreading out behind us, organized from recent to distant, a widening wake, the more distant the less textured, the less churning and relevant, the calmer and duller, with here and there a sparkle we can choose to look at . . . and then instantly that all changes and there isn't any present comporting itself toward the past, there is only the past laid out on a uniform sheet, the more distant parts as relevant and vivid as the comparatively more recent.

It's just so ugly, proportionately uglier and more aggressive, conceptually, the more spatially placid and egalitarian the layout. Because we used to look back together, needs of the moment making for the principle of selection and emphasis. With power over the *past, we were a proud, deserving aristocracy, holding dominion over a slave class—memories—that we could use to build for us. Now —a hideously mediocre democracy where every member gapes at me with as much right to appear and occupy space as every other member. And they're weak; the whole society is weaker now because the leadership has fallen, and a stratum that was meant to bear up an ongoing reign in which all significance ultimately resides— supplemented, you know, by the able underclass—is now buckling because it was never meant to bear the weight of being all there is, of having all the power.*

It's always, at the heart, the intractable problem of the suddenness, the being utterly blindsided. It is bottomlessly bizarre, and there's just no way to tame it. I still don't begin to understand it. Blindsided = blinded. And whenever I start to suspect that I am milking this whole experience, belaboring it for the sake of Being In It Longer, I recognize once again that I have yet to make my very first authentic response because I am still off balance, still blinking and nodding my head, still saying, "Like a balloon?," still shaking the doctor's hand. I can't remember exactly what happened when I went back to the people sitting in the waiting room at the Burlington hospital after I shook his hand. I think there were Kathy and Eric, Coleen, Schupack and Heidi? I think I first made the thumbs-down sign to Kathy, and then walked back among them, sat down, and that was it, we all just sat there. It was two o'clock.

I couldn't understand, only breathed. I didn't even gasp, as you might expect. That's one of the corollaries of being blindsided: having no useful angle on the situation, you never can appreciate it, and it's as though it has no angle on you either, which doesn't allow it to know you at all personally or to strike your body in such a way as to open up any specific wound. This would have happened to you, too, made you stumble around all this time, patting yourself in search of the wound, thinking, But wasn't I hit?

This had all been happening since about 8:45, when Eric called me and said he'd heard from another Goddard person that there was a car that looked like ours off Route 2 and that there was also an ambulance. That's all he said, and I got up and dealt with the dogs, putting Juno in her huge kennel, Romers in his, then pacing and standing by the window waiting for Coleen to come get me and take me up to the hospital. I thought about the huge spectrum of severity, the vanishingly remote chance that anything really terrible was going on, because it wasn't snowing or icing. It was like in the forties and gray, that's all. I stood by the window for a long time, and when I saw Coleen pull up out front I thought at first it was our car, because you remember she had just bought the same kind, same color. With her was another woman, but I won't say her name. As we drove up to the hospital, this other woman kept saying, "Oh, when I saw the car I just couldn't believe what it looked like, what a mess." That was the first I knew it was anything but minor. That's when I started to clench up for real, and I haven't relaxed yet. Much as I hate to indulge in this kind of maudlin, windy, and obscenely uncheckable abstraction, the kind that all letters to the dead (you're dead? I never say that) must include, my mind does try to suppose you in some state, and if so, it must be that in a fashion you have relaxed by now. Can't you help me do the same? I don't want to draw you back here against your will, but isn't just that much possible? How can I ever unclench on my own?

I've often thought of going back and back to that last look of

yours, finally getting clearer, making it like a citadel, you know?
Your eyes eventually coming to tutor me in calm and surety over
the years. But what about the fact that, prescient as your lingering
seemed, I just don't believe you knew?

You were blindsided too, but now you have been given your
angle, which is how you can manage to relax.

You remember that day—Valentine's Day, 1989—that Dad
came into the bookstore to show you the newspaper photo of a car
that looked like ours and had been in an accident. You knew I'd
been driving that morning, to my old high school to read a story to
students. (The road to the school was snowy, and I actually did skid
once pretty badly.) The injured driver was unidentified but the car
was registered to a Daniel Noel, my father's name (and maybe he'd
co-signed for the loan years before, who knew?). Dad was
frightened, though he was trying to be low-key for your sake. You
freaked out, called the hospital (same one that later took you in),
were told, "Yes, he was here but he checked out," the "he" meaning
me to you, of course. You ran back to our apartment at the bottom
of East State Street, and there I was, all unknowing, making for
you, believe it or not, a heart-shaped meat loaf in that pan I'd
bought for a quarter in New Haven.

Turned out to be that other Christopher Noel, the bad apple,
who had crashed.

And just the next month, in March, after we'd moved to the top
of East State Street, I was walking Romers one morning and you
were inside. I think it was a Saturday. On the sidewalk was the
lightest dusting of snow, treacherous, because it covered smooth ice.
Romers was pulling too hard as usual, and one moment I was
taking solid steps and the next moment—really, there was zero

interval, talk about being blindsided—I was already *trying to sit up* after *having slipped backwards and cracked my head. Weird little cartoons were playing in my head, swirling thought-forms and urgent abstract stories. I struggled to stand. My legs weren't working properly, like a giraffe or other specimen of Big Game after getting hit with the tranquilizer dart on* Wild Kingdom.

I made it inside, up the stairs, and in to you in the kitchen. You said, "Oh, my God, Buddy," all upset. I had blood running down the side of my face. You drove me up the long hill to the hospital, where I got four stitches.

I guess these two incidents have popped up because they're the best I've got for showing you being hit by me in trouble, and I can begin to extrapolate. But in those cases the danger was over long before you reached the point I reached when that woman started saying, "Oh, I can't believe how badly damaged that car *was . . . what a* mess."

In a way, though, you know better than I what it's like to lose us. In the first incident, disaster presented itself and then it withdrew. In the disappearance its shape could be seen; in the gap between what might have been and what was, the reality could be tasted; only as a possibility passing by did it have a flavor and a form. It left a trail in the air. If it had surrounded you and composed the molecules of you, lifted and shut your eyelids at the same time you chose to lift and shut your eyelids, how could you have been expected to notice and take it seriously? If a tree falls in the forest and you are a squirrel sleeping inside it until it hits . . . ?

One in the series of doctors who came in to brief me—the one who said all your other injuries were "small potatoes" next to your head injury—kept repeating, "It was a really bad hit."

What was it like? Your head, *Brig. I wonder, when I slipped on the sidewalk, how hard was that next to your "hit"—one-twelfth, one-fiftieth? I still have no way to measure the impact. The jewel of glass that Becky found in your date book gives me a pinpoint aperture into the land of that impact, but I can't really see inside yet. Is it humanly possible for me to share in what you went through, or will I be forever condescending, benightedly, slumming it? I never saw the car. (Sal and Peter went and gathered some of your things from it, maybe* our *things. I don't know what they found. Sal told me he still has a boxful and one of these days I will look.)*

You got to see my *head wound. When I saw you, the only problem was that you were just a little pale. Your wound was on the other side. If I'd rushed over and rolled your head, seen the wound, touched it, how would I be different right now? Not at all? Would that immediacy have been somehow domesticated, swallowed too and digested by the bottomless pit of merciful distance, healing, infectious, life-allowing, stunting? What if I had seen where they hastily, badly sewed you up after putting together your spleen? Isn't it strange that you even turned out to have a spleen? I'm sure I massaged it without knowing. I can picture your left leg, feel it, but of course I have no picture of it broken. I used to listen intently with my ear up to your heart and wonder how much stock I could put in such a capricious sound, how I could trust it to keep going these moments, much less through years. And yet it's what came through in good shape, going strong, not to blame, eager and able to keep your demanding, giddy brain nourished continuously for a lifetime.*

Oh Buddy Girl, I don't know what to tell you. What would you like to know? In this really stupid book, Death Does Not Part Us, *in which the author takes accounts of dreamed meetings with the departed as transparent evidence of experience after death, I "learned" that you folks don't know everything and often need communication from us folks.*

Yesterday I woke up to the loveliest snowfall. We got about five inches by early afternoon, and Romers and I went to Squeeky Park, this great big field right by us, and played with the tennis ball some, and then I made a tiny little snowball, plopped it down, and started rolling it with my pinkie and rolled it about sixty yards till it was as tall as my shoulder. It became the shape of a segment of a jelly roll and made the sound, rolling, of a faraway avalanche approaching. I wore myself out pushing. I stuck his green ball high up in the side, and Romers scaled this jelly roll, grabbed his ball, then fell back into the snow. Very funny. He's still the same dog you loved to describe: "his long velvet skull," and "the unfathomable soul that has come to be inside him, that makes such optimistic judgments, and that can never be distinctly revealed."

Today I've been finishing wrapping presents, having a good time at it, but really it's no good without you.

Here's one of the main problems I'm having: when I say "you," I'm not at all sure I know what I mean anymore. I know in life a person is like a sea, but you always have the port of their simple-remaining face and hands, etc.

You felt that "to write a memoir is to be seduced by the idea of persistence, of a single identity. What, in me, persists? Who am I always?" The trouble is that for me your core does not always, any longer, outplay your multiplicity, sickening as that must sound. I get lost, start to feel like one "in whom death is no longer a solid block but a network" (Stan Rice).

Remember when we left my father's apartment one night and it had snowed a little and the light from the moon came down in just the right way to make the car sparkle crazily, like trick photography for fresh-off-the-assembly-line? We kept saying, "Look, a new car! A brand-new car for us!"

I just remembered that the other day for the first time. That business of first-time memories is wonderful and dreadful, in just about equal parts.

I used to think I could keep a list and sooner or later I'd get to the end. That seems infantile now. This time-release quality, though, helps me understand why it's so impossible to gather you together and lean into you, like that snowball.

Poor Mark Twain had kids and a wife drop like flies. Writing about how it was after one daughter, Susy, suddenly went, he says that, in the beginning,

> *the mind has a dim sense of vast loss—that is all. It will take mind and memory months and possibly years to know the whole extent of the loss. A man's house burns down. The smoking wreckage represents only a ruined home that was dear through years of use and pleasant associations. By and by, as the days and weeks go on, first he misses this, then that, then the other thing. And when he casts about for it he finds that it was in that house. Always it is an essential—there was but one of its kind. It cannot be replaced . . . . He did not realize that it was an essential when he had it; he only discovers it now when he finds himself balked, hampered, by its absence.*

In the novel Housekeeping *(did you read that? I think you did),* *Marilynne Robinson touches on this many-ness problem by saying, about the mother's death,* "She left us and broke the family and the sorrow was released and we saw its wings and saw it fly a thousand ways into the hills." *And a little later, another passage you'll like: sisters Sylvie and Ruth are burning magazines; Ruth watches them begin* "to swell and warp and to page themselves. . . . It had never occurred to me that words, too, must be salvaged, though when I thought about it, it seemed obvious. It was absurd to think that things were held in place, are held in place, by a web of words." *Robinson's pointing to two contradictory things here, right?—to the obviousness and to the absurdity of words' cohesive power, and I also feel split. Words are blocking my way to you, like a swarm of flies, but of course we love them and they have in no small sense made us and fixed us in place for ourselves and each other, as you say in your essay on memoir:*

> *Why am I more fully alive, more engaged by life when I write, and in fuller possession of myself, than at any other time? . . . [The] effort to articulate what it is to experience my being is my chief joy in life.*

I feel so sad with that, I guess because the effort is the joy, the articulation is, not what's left behind, and language enlivens most as we press ahead and say more. It's bitter to read you without you, I kind of hate it in fact. Would you rather I loved it? But I know how sharp and unsatisfied you are, how you'd revise forever. Everything is freighted down with your not pressing ahead.

Oh, maybe looking back at your letters, at last, will feel different. I plan to read them down in the jungle, in February.

You wouldn't have wanted to go there; at least whenever we talked about South America you said, No thanks, too many bugs. After losing his wife Margaret suddenly in a fall, Edmund Wilson felt as I have often felt, thoroughly grudging.

> *Her death which deprived her of the things we have in life made them seem worthless to me—I couldn't enjoy them so much because they were things which could be spoiled for her and taken away from her. A loyalty to her had made me less loyal to life itself. . . . Satisfactions—books, love-making, drinking, talking, enjoyment of sensations—were not serious since they could be cut off from someone as fine and serious as she. . . . Why should you accept something which has been taken away from someone who deserved it so much— your true comradeship with her, true solidarity with what she represents for you that is noble, is to challenge life. . . .*

That's why I'm going to Belize.

I just stopped and let Romers go out back to pee. It's past 1:30 A.M., raining, ruining all the snow. Tomorrow morning, I'm going to wake up, finish packing, have breakfast with Joy, hand the travel agent twenty-two crisp hundred-dollar bills, and then take off for Vermont, home for Christmas. We're supposed to have a blizzard, six to twelve inches, and everyone's been urging me to drive up today instead, but I kind of want to go into the teeth of it. Remember how you always wanted more snow; you were always disappointed by the amounts we got.

I'll be turning thirty-three in five days, can you believe it? I'd barely turned thirty-one last time you saw me. How old will I be when you see me again?

Eight minutes before I turned thirty, I woke up and scrawled a note. I was sleeping by myself in the TV room. Where were you, Philly? Anyway, it said:

> *6:32 A.M. Still in my twenties, by gosh! Feels good, feels nice and early. Romers is sitting next to me scratching. What to say? I really love life and hate to see it marking itself along by any giant chunk, but mostly it's glorious because I am healthy with a house and lucky job and perfect Brigid (not in that order, of course) and vocation that's "big enough for all the art I can possibly put into it." Children, though, I am getting just about ready to meet you, already. Feeling almost antsy, tapping my foot, trying to see you walking up the road to me.*

I never showed that to you before.

Thank you so much for being perfect and making me feel so lucky. That's sappy, I know, but it's that time of year!

I guess I'll sign off now. Somebody *could let me know if somebody wanted more letters. I guess if somebody does not, then somebody doesn't care, I guess. I'm inviting you to drop by up in East Calais. The family could certainly use a breath of fresh air from you, we're choking here. Better yet, visit your mother, Brig. That would be the best.*

Second best, me. If you came, so that I felt you, that's all I'd wish for as a gift. Well, that and maybe some new shirts.

Merry Christmas, you know?

Your Boyster-Boy

Dear Mrs. ————,

I'm Christopher Noël, Brigid Clark's fiancé. I've always thought this would be an impossible letter to write, but now that I'm actually doing it, it's not so bad. I only hope it's not impossible or too difficult for you to read.

I want to say first of all that I hold no blame in my heart for you. I don't care about the technicalities of liability; that's all behind us now. What I'm saying is far more important: though I have remained sketchy, on purpose, in my knowledge of the details, I am certain that the accident occurred with no malice on your part, and the way I see it, the real culprit is a patch of ice, a hazard that can sneak up on anyone at all.

Maybe you don't need to hear this from me, but I thought that on the off chance it might help you, here on the two-year mark, I'd say it. We are both victims of this tragedy, and I've often wondered what you must be going through all these months. I haven't been ready until now to write you, but it feels good.

You may have been successful at putting the whole matter entirely out of your mind, and do not wish to be reminded. If that's the case, I'm sorry to have made it more difficult for you by making contact.

I have just one request, and if you're not able to meet it—if it's too painful or not your style—that's okay. For reasons that are difficult to describe, it would help me at this point to hear your side of the story, what the experience was like, emotionally and physically, for you, in as much detail as you can manage, before, during, and after the accident. It's been necessary for me so far to shield myself from the details, and if you can bring yourself to put down your story, I still might not be able to read it right away. But please know that if you go to the trouble of writing it, I will certainly read it, and though it will be painful for me, I am ready for that pain and I need what your story will provide, a greater closeness to and comprehension of what happened, from a human point of view, from the perspective of someone who was intimately involved. (I'm asking a few other people to write me their accounts too, so don't worry, you're not the only one.) Since I never saw Brigid again after she left the house that Tuesday morning (except for once, briefly, as she passed by me in the hospital on a stretcher), and since I didn't get to be with her, either at the accident site or in the hospitals, I feel that getting nearer to her and to the awful reality of what happened is the next best thing, being able to "be there" through the senses and hearts and minds of those who were actually there. I have been in constant communion with the Brigid I knew up till that day—with pictures and tapes and letters, etc. But more and more, I feel the need to be with her, also, right through to the end, which is why I'm asking for your help and the help of others.

Which brings me to my last point. Enclosed in the sealed envelope is a picture of Brigid. If you don't wish to open it, please just send it back to me. My thought in sending it was that since you and I are on opposite sides of the spectrum, since I have essentially nothing but memories of her before the accident, and since yours are only of it and after it, you might appreciate a picture from my side, to put alongside whatever you saw of her that day two years ago. If you do open it, and as you look at it, I want you to know

*that this was a deeply compassionate and realistic person, a
forgiving person with a keen sense of the sorrow and heartache that
life contains, a woman who understood better than most that things
do not always go according to plan. (Even if you do not open it, the
same holds true.) What I'm saying is, I hope you can let her smile
warm your heart.*

I wish you peace of mind.

Dear Mrs. ————,

You don't know me but my mother is a friend of your friend D.W., and I understand that you were present at the accident on January 28, two years ago.

I'm Christopher Noël, Brigid Clark's fiancé. I've come a long, difficult way since that day, and I've still got some distance to cover until I can feel that my life is back in focus, though of course I will never be free of grief. I have found it necessary all these months to keep my knowledge of the accident itself quite sketchy, but I've now reached the point at which I want to come closer to it. It feels odd to me that I was not there with Brigid at the accident.

What I am wondering, therefore, is whether you might be able to write me an account of your experience that morning. Please don't spare me anything just because you think I'd rather not know; I've not known for two years, but my desire now is to come as near as possible, finally, to having been there myself. I feel incomplete without this nearness, and though it will be painful, I am ready for that pain because in feeling it, I will be with Brigid, through you, in her hour of need. To whatever extent you are able to help, I will be forever grateful.

I must tell you in closing that in a strange way, I feel close to you already, which is why I can take the risk of asking you to do this difficult thing. Somebody told me that very day that a woman stayed with Brigid and held her hand; you'll never know the comfort this has given me all this while, and will continue to give me. To know your name, now, and to have this chance to thank you from the bottom of my heart for what you did, is a great privilege. As a small token, but one that I hope will bring you comfort as well, please accept the enclosed picture of Brigid. Place it alongside those unfortunate ones that you hold in your mind. May it come to outshine them.

five

At 7:05 A.M., my plane lifts off from Bradley International Airport near Hartford. The sun's just rising, turning the queasy, dank sky into lighter slate gray.

Joy and I woke up, in bed together, at 4:20, and what a chore it was to force myself to go. When you sign up for an adventure, you imagine it will be like boarding an amusement park ride, stepping on, and off you go, thrills taken care of. But in actuality, if you're doing it alone, you have to accomplish the adventure with your own muscle power and constant alert anxiety, very far from anyone who cherishes you, ever on the verge of making a giant misstep.

Joy drove me the forty-five minutes to the airport, joked with me, listened to my whining, assured me I'd soon be thrilled, and convinced me that, here in New England at least, I was vividly known and loved.

"Hey, what if it's a scam," she posed, "this whole idea that flying is safer than driving. I'll bet that's only if they lump you in with bad drivers, drunks. If you're not, probably flying **143** is *much more* dangerous. In fact, check all the victims of plane crashes and you'll find they were all *excellent* drivers!"

We bank to the east, angle upward over open ocean, clouds bunched salmony along the horizon. It is February 22, Brigid's and my eighth anniversary.

The last time I flew in an airplane I sat beside her, fifteen days before the accident; she and I were returning to Vermont from Los Angeles, where, the previous night, we'd taken plush seats at the world-famous Pantages Theatre in Hollywood for the Twelfth Annual ACE Awards.

Houselights dim; Dick Clark's voice has filled us in on what to expect, our cues for applause; stage lights dim; another voice, anonymous, enthusiastic, takes over for Dick's, welcomes a live nationwide television audience, introduces the evening's cohosts: stage lights come up bright, astonishing, lemony, on Cybill Shepherd and Danny Glover striding forward through the parting curtain, arm in arm.

Brigid and I glance at each other—well *this* is goofy—but instantly return our eyes up front. I almost cry. Brigid says, "I'm so tickled."

Roseanne and Tom Arnold present the award for our category, Children's Programming, and we lose to a show called "Harry the Dirty Dog," which means I don't get to deliver my extremely comical acceptance speech. (On the plane out, I'd massaged Brigid's calves and feet until she agreed to let me do the talking if we won.)

After the show, across the street from the theater, there is a gala. We step along actual red carpet, between cordons, past adoring fans trying to make out who we are, then we duck into a world kept under a big top tent. A brass band plays on a low platform stage; an acre of tables bears snacks and dinners laid out like in heaven; pineapples, coconuts, and small cakes are stacked in high pyramids; tuxedoed men and women carry trays of drinks, weave among palm tree-and-waterfall installations lit by their own upturned spots.

It's all absolutely free, because famous people get free things!

Brig and I acquire frozen strawberry daiquiris and platefuls of tiny sandwiches, grilled sausages, barbecued chicken wings, miniature pesto quiches, sit at a table by ourselves in one corner of the tent, overwhelmed. Of the famous, we agree, "We'll just sit here and let 'em come to *us*."

After about twenty-five minutes, two platefuls and two drinks each, we decide, "Hmmmm, let's go to *them*."

And so we circle the whole place five or six times, just soaking in the people and the quirky fact of our being here among them. Several times, our orbit takes us near comedians Richard Lewis and Steven Wright, huddled together talking and laughing earnestly by one of the tent's support poles. Each time, I struggle mightily with the temptation to break in and offer Steven Wright —free of charge!—two original jokes I've always thought he, in particular, would appreciate. ("Sometimes I go to restaurants and order out for things from home," and, "I've been thinking about peanut butter too much lately . . . it's sticking to the roof of my mind.")

On the plane home to Burlington, back into our stiff, humbling winter, I watched Brigid write in her journal:

People we saw at the gala after the ACE Awards: Beau Bridges, Lloyd Bridges, Graham Greene (from *Dances with Wolves*), Richard Lewis, Steven Wright, Jane Curtin, Charles Kimbrough (from *Murphy Brown*), Evander Holyfield (heavyweight champion of the world!), Dick Clark, Elliott Gould, Christine Lahti, Larry King, Christopher Reeve, Garry Shandling, Dr. Ruth Westheimer, John Lithgow.

Other highlights: Paula Poundstone won an award for her comedy special, which we've watched about 10 times (we cheered).

Roseanne and Tom Arnold announced our category during the ceremony and Tom A. actually said our title aloud on TV.

Leaving the gala, I was mistaken for Molly Ringwald by a pair of star seekers behind a barrier—Bud had been teasing me all day that he'd be mistaken for Kevin Costner and I'd be mistaken for Molly Ringwald—and then I *was*! We were walking down this red carpet between these rows of people with cameras, and I heard a woman say, "Is that Molly Ringwald?!" Buddy began to laugh, and I turned my head and shook it at her. "Yes it is!" she said. "Yes you are!" "I wish," I said. "I'd be rich, and I'm *not* rich." Very funny. Bud is gloating.

Midmorning, we cross the border into Florida, and here by my window in the last row of seats, I'm still bothered, as I have been since takeoff, by the continuous vibration of the jet engines right behind my head. Or I'm bothered less by the vibration—whose fluctuations don't sound healthy—than by the idea of continuousness itself, back to "occasionalism," to the question of the level of faith it's right to have in the world's sustaining itself from moment to moment. Why should these engines keep working, just because everybody around me is casually absorbed in newspapers and conversation? I can't decide whether to be more alarmed at knowing the secret about the easy interruptibility of series or at the way that even I, knowing what I know now, have gathered together so much faith already again that worrying about these engines strikes me as melodramatic, as merely teasing myself.

Florida spreads flat, mold green, lake dotted, down there. Many summers, Becky and I and Mom and Dad would walk along the paths and boardwalks of the Everglades; alligators crossed in front of us, amazingly propped and *trotting* on straightened legs; small lime-green lizards and larger striped ones, "skinks," marched up trees, spurted underneath our sneakers. I'd catch and hold them. The green ones I could put to sleep by turning on their backs and gently stroking their bellies. I loved lizards, oh! I could never get enough, and I had to admit they were even better—they might as well be dinosaurs!—than the dark green spotted frogs from the old days at the pond, which I'd doted over, wrapping my fist around their slender hips, breathing in the meatiness of algae, the bright smell of mud, laughing at the sudden strength in their attempts to pry themselves loose by pressing with their pudgy hands against the flesh of my curled thumb or index finger, staring into their globy eyes, which pulled in and away if you tried tapping them.

Amid hanging Spanish moss and rising cypress knees, we'd stop on bridges, gaze down into the water, and see long, cigar-shaped fish called, sensibly, gars, holding themselves stationary with tiny buzzing fins along their sides, and anhingas (or snakebirds), who swam just beneath the surface, only their long, bending necks stuck out. Sometimes we'd even see twelve-foot manatees cruising along and grazing, from beneath, with their great lips, on lily pads. In the trees and the sky were ibises, egrets, herons, turkey vultures, tiny, candy-colored finches, and once, sudden and serious across the top of the small valley we stood in —a giant snowy owl.

The humidity and fragrances and heavy, loamy odor every-where meant the pure, joyful crush of compressed possibility.

At Key West, we rode in a glass-bottom boat out past a wading flock of roseate spoonbills, and as we got into deeper water I was mesmerized by all the fish, large and small, and the rocky shelves and reefed chasms falling away below us. Once, the guide threw a ball overboard and two schools teamed up against each other for a game of football; the guide called the play-by-play over his microphone, and these fish actually attempted to advance the ball into each other's territory, made steals and various tricky plays.

Mom wakes Becky and me up in the middle of the night and leads us along the beach with a flashlight until we reach a spot where a massive sea turtle is laying and burying her eggs. I miss my bed, but the way the turtle is straining roots me—her wheezing, grains of sand stuck to mucusy eyes, staying there even when she blinks. Our flashlight bothers her, but she goes on with her job, until, with heartbreaking *ooofs!* she oars herself around and down through wet sand into warm, black waves.

Another time, Mom and I paddle out into the ocean on little inflatable rafts, dive down, using face masks and flippers. I can't hold my breath like she can, but I love going down in maybe ten feet of water, swimming next to her, seeing the soft, corrugated floor slope off below us into thick blue. We see lots of tiny fish, a few rays and flounders lying in the sand, and then we come face to face with a long barracuda, just hanging still in the sun. We empty our lungs of bubbles as we scream to the surface.

I feel these memories, really *feel* them, for the first time in years, as we glide in low over the marshland surrounding Miami.

west of
tea kettle

When the bluffingly reliable rockets boost us smoothly off the runway and south toward Central America, I'm visited again, though with awful brevity, by Brigid at my bedside, and this time I'm a layer nearer. I believe, though I can't be sure, that she's wearing her green corduroy pants.

Over Key West and then over empty ocean, it takes just an hour and a half until I can see the Yucatán peninsula, then the unbroken forests of northern Belize.

Touching down in Belize City, I notice occasional palm trees—just like in Florida, the kind with the long trunks and, at the top, coconuts and spiky ball of fronds—but not much in the way of lushness, and no flocks of toucans or troupes of howler monkeys running to greet me.

Waves of heat do rise dutifully from the tarmac, though, because it's eighty-five degrees and mostly sunny.

After customs, lugging my three heavy shoulder bags, I'm met in the parking lot by a man who calls my name, who tells me his is

Alwyn Smith. He's been sent by the hotel in San Ignacio to take me and a few others there, all the way across the country, two hours' drive on the Western Highway, one of the few paved roads.

Alwyn is a black man in his early fifties, extremely affable. We climb into his large, white van, start off with the windows shut and the air conditioner going, but when I tell him that where I'm from, one morning earlier this winter, it was thirty-eight degrees below zero, Fahrenheit, he suggests we open the windows, saying, "Clim-o-tize!"

After picking up three other North Americans at the domestic airport (a chummy Canadian couple and a woman in her late thirties), we stop at a refreshment stand to enjoy lackadaisical sodas. Why hurry? It's the middle of the afternoon and it's hot. I drink a tall bottle of Fanta orange, a brand no longer common at home but which I remember gulping as a boy.

Accelerating out of Belize City, Alwyn tells us that he's the father of twenty-two children, between the ages of four and twenty-six, and that at one point in his youth he was known far and wide as the fastest man in Belize.

On the Western Highway, we pass under banners welcoming the queen of England, who, it turns out, is visiting the country tomorrow. Alwyn says he doesn't care. She came here in 'eighty-five too, and he didn't go see her then.

When he was twelve years old, in 1952, the queen of England ascended to the throne, and became, thus, the queen of British Honduras as well, until 1974, when the country won its independence and reclaimed its original name. But England still funds projects here, and many Belizeans still think of Elizabeth as their queen.

The countryside is flat: dry grasses, bushes, palms, and pine trees, all shifting in the breeze. I'm intensely glad and surprised to have made it here at all, but really nothing about the land is very captivating for the first hour and twenty minutes, through and between the towns of Hattieville, La Democracia, Cotton Tree, Roaring Creek, Camelot.

What does reach and handle my heart, though, are tiny children walking along the roadside, in groups and singly, with cunning backpacks and clean school uniforms, powder blue, maroon, butterscotch. The clock on the dashboard shows it's just after three, the end of the school day; these kids are walking home.

Some little girls carry colorful umbrellas against the sun, and though their faces could well be *predicted* to slay me, as they turn to my window, they do. Some are black as black licorice, some the most remarkable deep reddish chestnut shade, with large, dark, far-set eyes and the sort of olden nose we're used to seeing carved in stone. Alwyn confirms that these are indeed Mayan children, and the darker ones Creole—the two major ethnic groups in Belize.

Their houses kill me too: little square structures on stilts, not because of flooding, Alwyn tells me, but because it's cooler that way. Some are ugly, made of cinder blocks, some wooden with dried-palm thatching for roofs. Some have walls that go only up to one's waist, for living alfresco. There are yards with cattle grazing, tied to palms or mimosa trees or stakes, or just loose, ordinary cows and impressive long-horned steer-type creatures, then horses and donkeys, and here and there a bright white egret hangs around, on the back of one or waiting by its grazing head.

Many of the porches and windows and front stoops show relaxing women and children, and older children holding younger—a very common sight already, which has a strangely moving effect on me—who watch us pass and quite often smile and wave, seeming genuinely happy to see us, which shocks me.

Outside a small-scale grocery store, a chalkboard stands in the gravel, and on it is scrawled a greeting to the queen.

And yes, there are flowers, bushes of them, sprays of them, trees of them, in all the colors but especially yellow and ruby-red, and sniffing the air restores my faith in the three-dimensionality of fragrance.

I hang my face out the window, in the hot sun and streaming summer, and flash onto a twilight in May or June years ago when Brigid stuck her head and shoulders out the window while I drove along a road in Vermont. Those metallic nighttime bugs were blaring from the fields we passed, the air was the drinkable kind, warm and cool at the same time, and full of earth, and she rode like that for long minutes, visiting me back inside just once to say she felt exactly like a child again.

But it's not until after we speed under a white banner whose red letters read, WELCOME TO HER MAJESTY QUEEN ELIZABETH II AND THE DUKE OF EDINBURGH TO THE VILLAGE OF TEA KETTLE, that the road gets much windier and up-and-down, and the land itself starts to ensnare and boss me. Dramatically angular hills, but, unlike Vermont's, mostly nude except for vivid green grass and a different kind of palm tree now—a brief trunk and fronds that start rising at my height (probably) and then fountain up and out, reaching thirty or forty feet into the sky. And here and there the hint of jungle, thicker groups of these palms and other trees and vines—actual vines!—stretching off into the distance.

Among these marvels, and more large-bowled flowers, tucked into tight clefts above us in the hills, more of those stilt houses, tinier-looking now because of being tucked, and moving about, safe inside their lives, the older children, boys as well as girls, carrying beensy siblings on their hips, on their shoulders, dogs sleeping or sitting or jumping, mothers cleaning up or hanging clothes or doing something I can't figure out in the three seconds during which their world is exposed to me. I see one house with two green parrots bobbing on the front-porch railing.

I too am tucked, tucked in green; I take a moment to realize I'm pleased, pleased, pleased, staring out the window with my mouth open. Instead of being an earthworm twisting on a hook, I feel right now much more like an inchworm, composed of curiosity, at the end of a stick. The world seems vivid, rich, fertile, relaxed, and it occurs to me that this staring I'm doing now is every bit as obsessed as that which I do into space at home, but, instead of attempting to empty myself, I'm taking my *fill*, green-guzzling. And what's this? By no means often, but every fifty breaths or so I get a *round* one, a junior yawn.

Approaching San Ignacio, we pass through Ontario Village, Mount Hope, Unitedville, Georgeville, Central Farm, Norland, none lasting longer than twenty seconds: a little store, an Esso gas station, perhaps two side streets, perhaps one. More school-children, maybe a one-story cinder-block school building. Every-thing's one story. People ride old, clattery bikes.

But I'm still much more excited by what goes on between villages. Over and over, my eyes light on hills, fields, forests that remind me of Vermont's for an instant and then trip my mind: "These are hills and fields and forests, yes, but not so fast—not yours at all!"

All these blasts of difference remind me of something my mother's college roommate Bette told me recently: When her husband Tony died and she spent that year sobbing, every day, as she rode to and from work on the train, she knew he remained with her but, as she told herself: "No daily newness from him now."

Down low in my stomach, just where I've felt that lava rising in the past, is a lighter, sparkly, unmistakable sensation I recognize as none other than . . . *glee.* I wonder, can an adventure such as this call forth the lava (as it was designed to) but in the form of glee, converting it, like lead into gold?

a tree of magpies

San Ignacio is a lovely town of eight or nine thousand, many of whom are milling about on foot or bicycles as we arrive, some shouting, teasing each other; others stand or sit on front porches, relaxing, drinking sodas from bottles; and yes, the uniformed schoolchildren, boys and girls, Mayan and Creole, still insist on blanking my mind and chest of all else whenever they look at me!

Most of these folks seem to know Alwyn well; they wave back to him when he calls their names, smiling and rolling their eyes with the admiration due a fine clown. He loves it here; it's the place of his birth, and he's remained his whole life. All his children live here, he says, though I still find it hard to believe he sired twenty-two in twenty-two years.

Laid out on a series of high bluffs along the Macal River, San Ignacio seems at first much more centralized beside this modest waterway where women wash clothes and kids: wide streets and a central square with benches and a large gazebo; many two- and three-story wood-frame buildings for apartments and offices; fascinating backyards with dogs and chickens crowded into them; frequent tall, mighty trees with small, sharp leaves; a basketball court with boys playing on it, the basket rims with no nets; several semifancy hotels and small, far-from-fancy restaurants; dirt roads proceeding upward into hills that rise on all sides, one of which, looming right over the town, is topped by a thicket of trees and vines. Alwyn tells us that inside that thicket is an ancient Mayan site called Cahal Pech.

My hotel is nearby, but I choose to keep riding as we deliver the Canadians up a long, red-clay "driveway" to their lodge. It takes us more than twenty minutes to make it the three and a half miles because the road is ludicrously cratered, rocky, steep. I'm breathless, soaring with earthliness; the glee sparkling in me turns even sharper now that I'm forging into hills that grabbed me even from a distance. Left and right are, of course, still further hills, velvety or sparsely treed, and close by the road those giant, fountaining palms again, here seeming *fifty* feet tall (Alwyn tells me they are called cohune palms), flowering trees and bushes, stony fields with black and brown cattle, snowy egrets attending them. A cow blocks our way for a minute. Sometimes there are orange and lime groves, and then a grove of short, twisty trees Alwyn says are cashews.

We stay for half an hour at the lodge, which is impressively landscaped, has cabins and walkways and platforms that look down on the river far below (shallow, pebbled, snaking off through crazy botanical riches) and across and far *up* at giddying, sheer rock cliffs. I stand next to Alwyn at a railing and ask, "So where are the monkeys?"

"Oh, you can *find* them."

• • •

My hotel room is spartan and dark. Over the bed, on the beige-painted cinder-block wall, hangs a small framed rendering of a tapir, Belize's national animal, which my guidebook tells me can grow "as large as 650 pounds, sporting a long upper lip and splayed toes, covered with hairless ashen skin, and boasting characteristics of both the pig and the cow."

At dusk, I walk down the hill into town and through and out the other side, past houses and along a dirt road into a field. Kind-eyed people take looks at me, as do chickens and dogs and horses and mules, none knowing what I've come for, about the conversion of lava. The air's a marvel, slack and coiled at once.

On my way back, at the edge of town, I come to a tall, spreading tree of a variety unknown to me; it is not, however, unknown to five or ten thousand magpies, all fighting for space in its branches. And shrieking! I mean it! They take my ears away from me almost traumatically, and I stand under them for a long time. It gets dark, but they keep brightly disagreeing; none has a reserved bone in her/his tall, butler-straight body, long, black paddle-tails flicking up and down: "And that's *another* thing!" I check around inside myself, but despite the new glee, I must say, No, afraid not, can't shriek. They've got me there.

After eating at a table by myself in Eva's Restaurant, where speakers emit songs like "Mr. Tambourine Man," after devouring a heaping plate of "spicy rice and vegetables," dashing too much hot sauce onto it so that I must swig two Belikins (Belize's own beer), I return to my room and fill the bathtub with the warmest water I can conjure from the faucet.

Naked, scrubbing with a hotel washcloth, I notice something else that this new kind of excitement is letting me feel, besides strangely wide awake: out in the hallway there are now and then sudden loud noises (things banging, people calling out . . . the staff making ready for the queen of England, who is to stay here as well), and instead of contracting as if slapped, as I'd expect, I find I feel poked—as in being poked *fun* at—like a child pleasantly toyed with.

Also, I drape the washcloth down my back, from just below the nape of my neck, and remember this is something Brigid and I used to do for each other while, occasionally, washing each other's hair, to make the washee less chilly in between warm rinsings out of a large plastic cup. The one doing the shampooing was called the "poozer," and the washcloth, the "pooz cape." This visitation hits me—surprise, surprise—not with that age-old cabbage chest but with a silly sort of jelly-belly flopping.

I lie back and open a shiny new book, the *Popol Vuh*, the Mayan creation myth my father suggested I read here, where it was composed long before anyone who looked like me or Brigid or the queen of England had ever laid eyes on a cohune palm. I add some more tepid water, and the world begins:

> Now it still ripples, now it still murmurs, ripples, it still sighs, still hums, and it is empty under the sky. There is not yet one person, one animal, bird, fish, crab, tree, rock, hollow, canyon, meadow, forest. Only the sky alone is there; the face of the earth is not clear. Only the sea alone is pooled under all the sky; there is nothing whatever gathered together. It is at rest; not a single thing stirs. It is held back, kept at rest under the sky. Whatever there is that might be is simply not there . . . only murmurs, ripples, in the dark, in the night. Only the Maker, Modeler alone, Sovereign Plumed Serpent, the Bearers, Begetters are in the water, a glittering light. They are there, they are enclosed in quetzal feathers, in blue-green . . .

My jelly-belly draws together, tightens, starts to clench, as these figures confer, "worried," uncertain how to proceed:

> Then it was clear, then they reached accord in the light, and then humanity was clear . . . the generation of trees, of bushes, and the growth of life, of humankind, in the blackness, in the early dawn . . .

After making "the deer, birds, pumas, jaguars, serpents," and so on, they turn to humankind:

So then comes the building and working with earth and mud.
They made a body, but it didn't look good to them. It was just sepa-
rating, just crumbling, just loosening, just softening, just disinte-
grating, and just dissolving. Its head wouldn't turn, either. Its face
was just lopsided, its face was just twisted. It couldn't look around. It
talked at first, but senselessly. It was quickly dissolving in the water.

"It won't last," the mason and the sculptor said then. "It seems
to be dwindling away, so let it just dwindle. It can't walk and it
can't multiply, so let it be merely a thought."

Next they try carving people out of wood, "manikins . . .
human in looks and human in speech," but they fail:

> . . . just an experiment and just a cutout for humankind. They
> were talking at first but their faces were dry. They were not yet
> developed in the legs and arms. They had no blood, no lymph.
> They had no sweat, no fat. Their complexions were dry, their faces
> were crusty. They flailed their legs and arms, their bodies were
> deformed. . . . [And so] there came a humiliation, destruction, and
> demolition. . . . A great flood was made; it came down on the
> heads of the manikins, woodcarvings. . . . There came a rain of
> resin from the sky. There came the one named Gouger of Faces:
> he gouged out their eyeballs. There came Sudden Bloodletter; he
> snapped off their heads. There came Crunching Jaguar; he ate
> their flesh. There came Tearing Jaguar; he tore them open. They
> were pounded down to the bones and tendons, smashed and pul-
> verized even to the bones. . . .
>
> They want to climb up on the houses, but they fall as the houses
> collapse.
>
> They want to climb the trees; they're thrown off by the trees.
>
> They want to get inside caves, but the caves slam shut in their
> faces.
>
> Such was the scattering of the human work, the human design.
> The people were ground down, overthrown. The mouths and faces
> of all of them were destroyed and crushed. And it used to be said
> that the monkeys in the forests today are a sign of this.

In bed, later, homesick, I turn for comfort to the first in the series of letters Brigid sent me while I was at the MacDowell Colony writing for thirty days in April and May 1991. I've brought the red binder of her correspondence with me. As the letter opens, she's sitting in the living room with our two dogs, Juno and Romeo, and our cat, North:

> *I am very lightheaded at the moment, sitting on the couch as the dogs ricochet around the living room. Juno just now is very anxious to get her freckled snout in on this letter. Now she is chewing at the base of her spine. . . . And Romers has just done a fan dance with his tail and his rolly eyes and has got Juno wrestling again. Northrup, it is safe to conjecture, is moping by the refrigerator. As you can see, things are very similar to the good old days when you lived here.*

On and on it goes, updating me on the minutiae of her day and evening—"Then I lay in the tub and read some more and contemplated my pale, pale belly . . ."—and she closes, "Hey, it's REALLY quiet here, without my Boyster. When are you coming home, anyways? It's sad here. Boo hoo. I hope you're getting work done. Remember—I'll be taking this all out on you later. You can call me any time. *Any* time at all. Bye, Boyst. I love you." It's a pleasant surprise to feel just humbly swaddled by this first foray into The Letters, so I push on to the second, which is all about J.A., one of Brigid's high school teachers, more than twenty years her senior, with whom she had a two-year relationship from age seventeen to nineteen. This relationship hung as a perpetual shadow over our own. She's writing me on April 17 to say she's just received from him, after a long silence, what is

> *in essence a one-page autobiography, written pretty closely on both sides of the page, and yikes it's scary. . . . I will enclose a copy. . . .*

When I read this letter, it shook me up a lot. It's very raw. And I wondered if I wasn't pitting myself against evil, or Satan, or something, because no matter how hard I try to deal with this man, he comes back at me with something very real and heartbreaking.

I remember her taking me for a walk on the grounds of her high school one day, in suburban Philadelphia, pointing through a window to the room in which he first told her he was in love with her. She said those walls rippled, and she had to put a hand out to steady herself. We climbed up the hill at the top of which, on her seventeenth birthday, he first kissed her. We followed the cross-country course where, to be alone, they'd run together after school, and she showed me a marshy place off to one side where she'd often go to wait for him. Other times, she'd wait in a nearby cemetery, sometimes for hours, sometimes in the rain, and he might or might not appear, depending on whether he'd been able to disentangle himself from his wife and children; and if he did, they would make love right there, quickly, she always terribly nervous they'd be stumbled upon.

The secrecy factor was deepened by the fact that Brigid's mother was the school librarian, and constantly suspected this was going on; but to protect J.A., and to keep at bay the threat of intrusion, Brigid raised a seamless front of denial and deception (which lasted, incidentally, until the Christmas just before the accident, when she finally confirmed her mother's worst fears and they had a talk, the first of what would need to be many).

He was a brilliant, flamboyant, stormy teacher, friend to students, enemy of a stodgy administration, a self-important man whom Brigid at that age took to be a Great Soul in need of soothing, of rescue from his Suffering. He felt he was underappreciated at this school, should have been a college professor, loathed himself, would threaten suicide. Once, on a Friday, sitting at his desk, he told her that he had a gun in the drawer and that by the end of the weekend he'd shoot himself but that she mustn't breathe a word of it. She couldn't call him at home, of course, so she carried this secret on her shoulders until Monday morning, when she found him at school safe and sound, his mood much improved.

Everything was always on his terms, since he had the career and family hanging in the balance. He'd set meeting times and places, change the plans on a dime, resent any demands she might make on his time. When she went off to college, Brig would check her mailbox three and four times a day, and once every six or eight weeks would find a short, cryptic note from him. During her first two years at Yale—the second being after she'd ended the relationship—she felt, as she said, like "a bombed-out ruin," barely able to concentrate, usually too depressed to make and keep friends.

In the last year of her life, her efforts at exorcism included writing him and speaking to him a few times on the phone. Once, he called her at work and they had their frankest discussion ever. When she asked him why he'd been so angry, why he preyed upon one who was so clearly in need of immense amounts of approval, of being singled out by a powerful figure and deemed a princess, one who was in no position to know what was best for herself, his only response was to ask, "Well, why were you so *fucked-up?*"

Brigid often had nightmares in which he tracked her down in Vermont. And then, eight days before her accident,

I dreamed that I flew down to Florida to find J. I think I sought him out, meaning to shock him from my appearance, but what I recall from the dream is approaching him at a rendezvous in a big, urban parking-lot-type setting: multilayered garage, dim, empty, parking spaces marked out, squared cement pillars. As I walked toward him, so full of anxiety I could hardly look straight at him, those pillars drifted between us as I passed them. He was at first older looking, haggard, much more gray in his hair, and with a scruffy gray beard—kind of long and wild. But when I drew near and finally began to talk to him ... I ended up in an embrace with him—I believe we had sex. After that, we talked, and he sneered at me, saying the last time he'd heard from me I'd "just begun to learn to feel again. . . ." Ultimately, he got enraged, said he'd kill me—this may have been in response to a challenge or threat of mine—and pulled out a gun. He tried to fire it. I was screaming and completely panicked and it didn't work. He pulled out *another* gun, just to prove to me how planned and felt this was. . . . Somehow I got away, thanks to both guns not working.

Just below, in her journal, in the list of "ten scariest things" I quoted from earlier (Number 3: "Dying in an accident")—Number 7 is "Seeing J. again."

"He's just a person," Brigid wrote in a letter (never reciprocated) to a woman rumored to have also had an affair with him while in the ninth grade. "I know he's not merely destructive energy, but he has something of the mirage to him—now you see him, now you don't."

I grit my teeth and slide out of its protective plastic sleeve the Xerox of his cramped handwriting. In addition to much raving and complaining and sexual confession that I will not quote, the letter tells Brigid,

You were many things to me: the real safe haven in which I rested, the classroom intellect in which I took such delight, but above all the life which released life in me; was it just one more fantasy? Why did I feel so incredibly, intensely alive with joy, passion, terror, guilt, and so on? Never before (or after) was I so connected, so alert, so intensely alive with all receptors open, all systems 100% engaged!—I thought. But if so, how could I have been so blind to your real needs or at least to the prospect that I didn't really understand them, and should proceed, in what started as a friendship, with consummate caution! And now I'm hurting again; every day I summon you up (or do you just appear?) and say hello and relive it a little (one episode or another) and always end up apologizing to your image or shadow.

It's no wonder to me that even eight years after last laying eyes on the man, she still found herself ambivalent about categorizing him as a mere perpetrator of sexual abuse.

We'd entered therapy together largely because of the extensive fallout of this history on our relationship. This fallout is difficult to characterize, but one way to say it is that whatever in her needed, thrilled to, the passionate approval of such a Zeus-like figure, the rich drama of a situation that's forbidden and fated at once, could not be stirred again by me, a peer, a mere mortal.

In my hotel room now, long past bedtime, I resume her letter:

> What is it I'm having trouble resisting? He's real right now, for a little stretch. Maybe I'm just fascinated at this intimate look at his psyche. It's like being an anthropologist examining one of the last specimens of the Great White American Male. I have a real love of suffering, a giant reservoir of compassion and empathy in me waiting to be tapped into. But not everyone has access. . . . Maybe I can't stand the suffering of people like me, peers, flawed young people

staggering around stupidly, asking for help. It's gods I like to see suffer, gods I want to help. People I don't expect to be weak, but who are. . . . I think sometimes I'm afraid [our therapist] will rob me of subtlety, that he'll reduce me to a little pinhead parroting his theories . . . and that would be robbing me of my ability to be an artist, I suspect.

(Later, her mother decided the question in one way by writing to the superintendent of the school where J.A. was hired after leaving Philadelphia, explaining that Brigid was dead and that the family did not intend to pursue him for what he'd done to her, but that if there were any suspicions surrounding his current behavior, she would be able to furnish proof of his past dealings.)

But don't you think that in order to know life, and people, you should not shy away? But maybe I know this personality too well, or he knows me too well—I'm having trouble disarming him, and he keeps coming at me. . . .

I've been contemplating writing a story about J. from the point of view of his daughter, who [while we kissed and hugged] he leaned against the tree in the snow in her baby backpack when she was very small.

Though it pains me to say so, Brigid and I had a troubled sex life most of the time. The easiest, most simplistic way to put it is that I wanted to make love much more often than she did, and this asymmetry caused a lot of strife and heartache, spoken and unspoken; she told me many times that *she* missed her libido too, that its being "lost in space," as she put it, saddened her as much as it did me.

Another way to put it is that meeting J. in a foggy cemetery —even for fast, secret, weedy intercourse—was a transporting experience in a way that a straightforward, safe love relationship can never be. Nor did we ever succeed (and I'm part of this, of course) in evolving our own compensatingly rich erotic style or "language of passion," as we sometimes called it when trying to put our finger on what was lacking. Mostly, our power lay in being best playmates—after all, we called each other "Buddy." We were also lovers, but our lovership seldom managed to transcend the friendship.

I finish her letter of April 17, 1991: *"My head cold is still going strong, and I miss you very much. I wish you were home. I think you really are the best for me, a real man, a person to be grateful for."*

I turn out the light and lie here feeling the humid breeze wash over my body.

No.

What I just wrote is wrong, it's much too tame and tidy. Saying "we were also lovers, but our lovership seldom managed to transcend our friendship" is stilted and could apply equally to just *any* friends who occasionally cross that line for the hell of it. Our struggle wasn't like that at all. Everything hung in the balance.

At the beginning of the world, those "cutouts," those "manikins," ached to become human beings, because otherwise they knew they were lost and gone.

The breeze hasn't stopped touching me gently—my hair, face, and shoulders—and I'm wishing she could have been free to want to touch this body as much as I wanted to touch hers, wishing I could scream out this horrible complaint like those forthright magpies.

I try to empty myself and draw a round breath, but no luck; I'm breathing like a cutout.

What an elaborately difficult thing, to be a creature in the world. Because here's more: into the mix was Brigid's powerful disinclination to "be with" her *own* body. She felt fat, no matter how much I, and others, disagreed. She'd diet. We'd go running. For Christmas, the last one, I got her a stepper machine and one of those ski-motion machines, for winter workouts. The stepper she loved and was using religiously. In her shoulder bag, taken out of the car, was found an orange she was planning to eat for lunch that day. She'd go through better phases in her relationship to her body, but to some extent she and it were always at odds; she told me she didn't feel *in it* during sex; she told me, sometimes, that she wished vehemently she could just hack away portions of her hips and thighs and calves, that she looked deformed. This is why it disturbs me so much to imagine her unable to hide her legs from the onlookers after the accident. I can remember well how happy she'd get when, after a period of regular exercise, she'd notice and point out to me a bit of muscular definition in those legs.

She explained vividly to me one night—when I couldn't keep my feeling unwanted quiet anymore—that she used to distinctly separate from her physical self during those outdoor encounters with J. (never once in a bed), not hovering above the scene watching, but just not viscerally present, getting no sexual satisfaction at all. Somehow, though, she was *emotionally* more than satisfied. She went on to admit to me, crying, that a version of the same physical departure went on when we slept together, that she didn't really feel inside the experience.

I tried not to take it personally, but I didn't know how to help, because the bottom line seemed to be that she saw her body, especially her lower half, as a detestable thing, even if I'd kiss it, over and over. This later allowed me to accept as a certain kind of mercy the family's decision to cremate her.

Ninety-nine point nine percent of the time, we avoided this whole territory, because it made us sad as stones, and because I *did*, of course, take it personally. Sometimes, today, I even find myself ruefully thanking Brigid for not having wanted me. "Maybe that's why you lost me, ever think of *that*? *Joy* wants me!" Is *this* why I find I'm unable to fantasize about her, or is it only because she's dead?

What worked best to lighten this burden was plain old child-like play. Brigid was at once the saddest and the happiest person I have ever known. One of our first times together, as she tells it,

> . . . we walked in the snow by a river for hours. It was so fascinating and so funny, I felt like Lou Reed on the way to East Rock and I felt like Charlie Chaplin on the way back. But I mostly felt like I was five years old again, because my bod was hung right for a change and because I felt so good for no résumé-related reason. "You say you feel like you're five, how's that?" said Chris Noël. And I told him it was because I was walking different, like they do. He wanted to know how, so I took a few broad, longish, rotund little steps and I said, "They walk with a sense of well-being, like this, see?"

I'm falling asleep, while, out in the hallway, hotel workers still drag furniture and clean. At first, the queen's being on her way excited me like a kid. But there are troubles in the idea. Didn't J.A. make Brigid feel like a princess in order to pluck her out of the many? Didn't English civilization take colonies like this one *I'm* now using for my own purposes? Hasn't the British government been slaughtering and dominating the Irish, Brigid's ancestors, for centuries?

The citizens of Belize gained their independence in 1974, yet the queen still visits, and they still want her to. Thousands of people will turn out in the San Ignacio town square tomorrow afternoon, curious to see for themselves the incarnation of what, for a long time, stood for civilization itself, what stands now for a civilization on the decline. Many will be Mayans, of course, the very ones whose ancestors are helping me to see, tonight, that in each life humanity must try itself out again, and fail, calling down, in some form, the floodwaters. That leaves me thinking of Brigid's ashes, of my own body struggling to live again, as

> just an experiment and just a cutout for humankind. . . . They flailed their legs and arms, their bodies were deformed. . . . [And so] there came a humiliation, destruction, and demolition. . . .

One morning in the spring of 1992, a couple of months after the accident, another former teacher of Brigid's called me. It seemed the superintendent of J.A.'s school had showed him Brigid's mother's letter, and a few days later J. went out to his boat, put a gun to his head, and pulled the trigger.

"Imperfect things can be perfect," Brigid wrote in her journal in March 1989.

Grief gave birth to the adult me, and for some time I felt bound to it, as though by an umbilical cord. Only by rejuvenating the child-me have I been able to free myself from grief and feel joy again, purely.

Joy has less texture than grief. Joy without grief is dim. Grief necessarily entails joy, and it makes experience, the experience of grief and life simultaneously, sublime. Joy is a childhood emotion. Grief is a gift that accompanies the loss of innocence. Which is preferable?

Passion makes the world pale, is its own reality within reality. It is the source of my most fertile moments in life. Passion and Childhood Joy are alike in their capacity to remain tangible, to engender images.

I think it is important to laugh at humanness. It seems like a virtue to me. Insight into our sameness and vulnerability makes me happy, to my soul.

I want to know my own mind.

I want to learn to love paradox.

Early in the morning, I lie still, smelling the same heavy but animate air, preserved and carried over from yesterday. Though it smells heavy, it taps and slides lightly across my closed eyelids—a very exact sensation, coming back to me from a long time away. What am I remembering? This motion on the outside meeting bottled excitement within me, making the lids themselves the site of imminence, this skin getting more from this breeze than other skin can, as if my eyes are somehow *more open* like this than if they were really open. It hits me: This is just how I'd feel at the beginning of summer vacation, waking up those mornings, the whole thing stretching out before me, offering no end of possibility.

> Now it still ripples, now it still murmurs, ripples, it still sighs, still hums, and it is empty under the sky.

Two hours later, I'm in the back of a pickup that's racing over terrible dirt roads toward the border of Guatemala. It's a bright, hot, beautiful day. The truck is driven by Mar-   **173** guerite Beevis, part owner, with her husband, of the Mountain Equestrian Trails Camp, at the edge of the rain forest, where I'll be staying for the next three days. In the back with me are her four smiling children—Trevor, age eight, Heather, eleven, Lacy, fourteen, and Aaron, fifteen.

After buying some supplies—horse blankets, ropes, etcetera —in a nearby Guatemalan market town, we race back to San Ignacio, arriving a minute and a half before the queen and duke finish their appearance, step down from the platform, get into their limousine, and zoom up the hill to "my" hotel. Just in time, at the back of a lake of people, many of whom carry floral-print or white or black umbrellas, I stand on tiptoe, snap a few pictures over their heads, am not sure but think I catch a glimpse of Her Majesty (wearing a smart beige cap), not cleanly but filtered through bustle, and then I quickly become much more engrossed in crowd watching. Tightly knit bands of schoolchildren in those matching outfits weave this way and that, some holding hands, some biting into raspberry Popsicles. There is a brass band playing a lively tune on a circular stand, and within the general upbeat hubbub I notice in the faces the stillness of anticlimax. Apparently, She didn't say a word, just waved that modest wave of Hers. Up on the festooned stage, in simple folding chairs lately occupied by members of the official entourage, sit a couple of men, ordinary folk, staring sadly into space. One girl, probably ten or eleven, strides along the pavement toward me in a rust-colored uniform, a bright red Popsicle jutting from her left hand, and in a tone that's a perfect blend of scorn and leftover zeal, she says to nobody in particular, "Roy-al-tay!"

. . .

Another half hour along an even worse rock-dirt road takes our truckload to the Beevises' camp; I am shown to my blue tent in the forest. Higher-paying customers stay in comfy cabanas across the field near the main building, an open-walled, dried-palm-frond-roofed structure where there's a bar and tables for the guests' breakfast and dinner.

Heather shows me around the sprawling grounds—horse pens and stalls; large flowering trees; new campsites being cleared and trimmed, cooking pits dug, water lines laid; several ramshackle buildings where the cooking is done; a cat—Ponchita—who yips like a dog; the tiny, bug-eyed dog Risa, who if you hold her in your palm and blow just once into her face will rub her snout on both sides with her paws for about twenty-five seconds; high green ridges off to the north; many intriguing pathways leading into "the bush"; and perched on a near hill overlooking the whole place, the Beevises' circular home with great big windows and a porch that runs all the way around. They came here from Texas four years ago.

We sit beside a banana tree, and Heather talks about the book she wants to write, about a girl lost in the jungle; I talk about the novel I'm trying to write called *Must Warn Others!,* a comedy about an oceanographer obsessed by an elusive subspecies of tuna, a genetic engineer down and out in a labyrinthine biotech firm, and a horror writer/widower who, in losing his wife, has lost the capacity to scare himself; they all want life on earth to be stranger and more astonishing than it is, and though they never know one another, they inadvertently conspire to bring this about. "I guess," I say, "it's also a look at the lighter side of grief." After a pause, Heather coughs and says, "I've never gotten lost in the jungle, not really, so I'll have to make that part up."

Soon, I retreat to my tent for a couple of hours. I'm beginning to experience a backlash, homesickness rising and meeting with the recollection that, oh yeah, I don't have a home anymore. I unpack, putter around, try to read another Brigid letter, get too sad, try to write about this, get too sad even for that.

I force myself to visit the nearby outhouse, which is just built and has never been used. I sink onto and into its fifteen-inch hole, which grabs the cheeks with its piney circumference and kindly retracts your anus for you.

In the tent again, it strikes me why I am heart-sunk in this particular new way: I am sick with envy of the vividness and solidity of the history this family is making here at the Mountain Equestrian Trails Camp. I don't envy this choice of livelihood but the vividness itself, the *fact* of history being made *anywhere* so distinctly. I flash back onto the way Heather's wrists bent, during the tour, to let her hands display the various features of her world, the unhidden, floppy pride in such very young wrists. She told me that she knew some kids wouldn't appreciate living here, that they'd be bored or lonely, but not her; "I know I'm lucky," she said as her hands uncurled over and over, palms toward new projects, old favorite spots, large, shallow pond stuffed with weeds (not unlike my old frogpond!), hands then just offered out and up, by her ribs, as she explained some plans the family had for the future. She petted the dog and cat, picked for me dark green Jamaican oranges from a tree, warning me how bitter they are, grinning as I bit in: "Don't say I didn't warn you."

So, this envy can hit even at the very threshold of two hundred miles of uninterrupted, surging rain forest of the sort you have longed to explore ever since you can remember. Is it like this, is it exactly the high drama of this place that throws into relief, craftily, the even lovelier drama, writ small within it, in the mere wrist-happy liking of daily life?

At dinner I sit at the children's table, garnering amused looks from the grown-ups. But it's a tonic, talking with them. Over fried chicken, rice, and broccoli, Heather's sister, Lacy, tells me about the six-foot boa constrictor their brother Aaron found on the compost heap the other day. He had to chop its head off, because it could hurt us. Athena (pronounced "A-teen"), a nineteen-year-old Belizean woman who grew up down the road and keeps accounts here at the camp, is very perturbed that some of her childhood friends have let their lives go, taken to drinking all the time or having babies. She plans to wait to have children, she says, as if it's the height of prudence, "until I'm something like *twenty-five*."

Meagan Reading, the Beevis kids' nineteen-year-old tutor, astonishes us with a mental gift: She can photographically recall exactly what people were wearing at any given moment. I say, "Okay, eighth grade, Flag Day," and since she happens to have had a crush on one Keith Roberts, she does remember standing with her class in a circle around the flag and looking across at the young man: white button-up shirt, leather belt, red jeans. Can't say what shoes. Again and again, she stuns the table, telling each of the Beevis kids, and me, what we had on when she first laid eyes on us.

It is a very pleasant, summery evening. There are candles on the table, blazing chalky moonlight outside. I'm being myself, a good listener, asking sincere questions, cracking jokes. Round-faced, towheaded Trevor entertains us with rapid grins and non-sense sounds, a little monkey. We all relate recurring nightmares, earliest memories. Trevor has only recently grown too large to be picked up and carried.

I say, "Isn't that awful?"

"Yeah," he says. "It's bad when you lose some fun."

I teach Heather how to draw stars with five quick strokes of the pen, her hands and those famous wrists doing their best; then she tries me on some drawing riddles, connecting dots to make certain shapes without raising the pen off the paper.

I pull out a fifty-dollar bill and demonstrate my only "magic" trick, which is to pretend to rip the bill in half while producing a very convincing sound with my mouth. They are gloriously amazed, don't catch on. I bet they'll lie up the hill in their beds, later, wondering how on earth.

And how on earth does this evening with them cure my spell entirely? One firm link with a good kid, however brief, can freshen even me to the core; one sturdy glance between us sets me safely in a stone house I've called home for centuries.

I say good night and cross the field, lit by a moon that's approaching full. I step—foolishly sneakered, not booted—through tall grass that could easily host a deadly coral snake or fer-de-lance (a nocturnal pit viper), about which my guidebook warns, "There are many reliable reports in Belize of individuals who have died soon after stumbling on the animal in the bush.

. . . usually only the younger snakes are hot-headed enough to actually come after humans."

I reach my tent, laboriously get the kerosene lamp lit, then pay another visit to the presumptuous outhouse. On the way back, a firefly pulses just above me. Awww, good ole summertime friend . . . but when I train my flashlight beam on him, I shudder—he's at least three times too large to be fond of.

In a small concrete building up a hill from my tent, I take my clothes off and step into a shower stall whose water source is a hanging black bag designed to soak up the sun's heat during the day and give out warm water at night through its plastic nozzle.

Nope.

Trembling, shampoo congealing on my head instead of rinsing away, I realize I have stepped into the precise tremble of that notorious YMCA sleepover. I was nine years old, and it was supposed to be fun. Locked in the building overnight with at least a hundred other boys, all of whom relished this opportunity, wrestling and cackling and lobbing loud insults, forming bold alliances, not missing their mothers one ounce, I'd never before felt homesickness at such a pitch. All I remember is trying to lie low and endure the minutes. Late at night, while my legbones stung with fatigue and distance from my own bed, the counselors herded us into a bare, rugless room and projected onto the wall a film called *The Incredible Colossal Man*.

Radiation had made a scientist fifty feet tall and lonesome, so he rampaged through the countryside and into cities, and when people ran from him screaming, he'd be so hurt that he'd pick them up and eat them. All around me, boys were hooting. Some roared like the colossal man himself. At one point, he picked up a guy wearing green, popped him into his mouth, chewed him up, then spat him out; he landed on a sidewalk, up against a brick wall, making a horrible, mushy splat, like a wad of boiled spinach. At the end, the scientist died by throwing himself into power lines, calling out "Joyce!" (wife) as the electricity surged into him, taking him out of his misery.

We laid out our sleeping bags on the floor of the gymnasium. Hour after hour, I had to pee worse and worse, deep into the night after the rest had finally shut up and started breathing like gentle souls. I don't remember why I didn't know where the bathroom was or why I didn't ask one of the counselors. I guess they left to go to sleep themselves, or else I was just paralyzed.

At about four in the morning (I seem to remember a wall clock), I crawled to a garbage can and got a Coke bottle, brought it back to my sleeping bag, and carefully peed into it, almost filling it up.

In my tent, now, I am more nervous than I ought to be. For dessert there was lemon meringue pie, and I gulped down two pieces, even though sugar dissolves my peace of mind. Outside, I know it's not the heart of the Congo, but it is the actual edge of an actual jungle, and I can hear a stick break far away. I wince; closer sticks snap, and then a heavy body of some sort drags itself along through brush. When it gets to within twenty feet, it stops and is silent. "Is the monster here yet?"

So where is my red hot lava, spoiling for a mortal battle, when I need it?

As if peccaries (wild boars) and tapirs and the deadly snakes weren't enough, there are also pumas and jaguars in this forest, though I'm told they are extremely skittish, not at all likely to stalk a tent.

Still shaking a little from the shower, and from whatever has arrived outside my flimsy zippered door, I pull from its sleeve Brigid's letter number 3 and feel instant solidarity. Just the word *today* is a radiant blessing over me, out here.

> *Today I got so cold I burned all the twigs and chips that were left, and right now the stove is hot, but there's nothing left to burn. . . . My fingers really have been getting stiff at the keyboard—I feel like Dickens. Except, of course,* for *the keyboard. Maybe I will burn the dogs. . . .*
>
> *Today I had both kennels stacked in the doorway so I could print out in peace, and the dogs were cavorting around the house, and all of a sudden Romers leapt to the top of his own (the highest) kennel! I had been kicking them out regularly, so I turned in surprise and looked at him with a dawning disgust, but he was so perky and proud up there, his tail waving slightly, in anticipation, as it were, that I couldn't help but smile at him. He jumped down and I hugged and kissed him and told him he was a circus dog, yes he was, a real circus dog, and then Juno barrelled through and I told her she was also a circus dog, poor ungainly thing. . . . You probably have this kind of experience all the time, in the mornings, but not me, no sir, I'm out busting my* balls *to earn money for the family, that's* you, *buster, HEY. Look at me when I'm talkin' to you.*

By ten fifteen in the morning, I am back in the dark, aboard a rowboat on a river deep inside a mountain. Also in the boat is a couple from Chicago, Al and Sharon; and our guide is Jim, the Beevis kids' uncle, a quiet, wry, long-haired, appealing twenty-one-year-old who claims to still find this fun after fifty trips.

The cave is never more than twenty feet wide, the river ten to fifteen feet deep, and the rock ceiling varies from two to one hundred and fifty feet above us. When it's two, we all have to lie back with our shoulders on the seats while massive stalactite points or flatter formations brush slowly over us. Claustrophobia rises; it seems baldly insane to be squeezing through here *on water*. Soon, though, we sit up underneath sudden vaults; with our flashlights we can hunt out high rooms, follow along shelves and what seem to be pathways leading off to further chambers, into which we can only peek. With equipment, we could hike away up inside there, into the belly and head of this mountain.

We edge under several stone archways; Jim

tells us that on the top surface of one of them, the bones and belongings of a Mayan were discovered. Tremendous soft-ice-cream mounds hang over us left and right, some frosted with white crystals. Often, directly overhead, and high enough to gain momentum, monstrous stalactites hold their breath, and just when you think they could never really let loose and fall, your beam catches the jiggly image, on the river bottom, of a wrecked one just below.

Near the back of the cave, three-quarters of a mile from the sunny, viny mouth, a pumpkin—but tan and the size of a pumpkin to Thumbelina—rears out of the black. Most of the time, bats slice by our faces.

Yes, I am alive to all of this, rather objectively, in my mind, but I find I feel angry too, and I'm not sure why. This is an outrageous, extremely unlikely place to be, and for this reason, though unexpectedly, I resent it; I've tonged myself up and placed myself in here, so now here's where I *have* to be. I'm a trapped thing, and I'd be nowhere of the kind if it weren't for what's taken place on an average January morning; I wouldn't be trying to shock myself alive again, or be dreading the descent, next week, into the Blue Hole, easily a hundred times more dangerous than this.

This strange venom of resentment isn't, I believe, to be confused with the lava, because it doesn't feel formidable and like the heaving shoulders of life; instead it springs from the shocking discovery that shock therapy isn't guaranteed, that such drama can dramatically miss me. I'm cool, dense clay lumped here in a rowboat, with a dull, greasy film on me that smacks of bile.

The musty, clefted world I'm stuck inside could either collapse this second or remain perfectly intact till long after all four of us are dead of old age. I bet it was the very same in here at the separate moments Brigid and I were born. I don't care; nothing really succeeds in changing.

What's so disgusting about one's writing out and filling, *for oneself,* the prescription for adventure? There is something miserably circular going on. I'm using myself, providing for myself somehow sleazily. I remember how "smutty" I felt back at Christmastime. Is this sort of high-handed self-solicitude so different from the criminal sense of "solicitation"? Am I overstating the case? I've got to think this through.

At the back of the cave, we turn off all the lights and sit in the abounding dark for a minute, listening to several runnels splashing into our river; Jim tells us that's water coming from outside, says it sounds heavier than normal, and we amuse ourselves by speculating whether a big storm, whose rain might raise the river level and block our exit, has kicked up since we've been in here.

Back outside, the others paddle to shore, and I swim there from a rock at the mouth, about forty feet through murky turquoise water, water shared, a few miles downstream, by crocodiles.

While Jim washes and beaches the rowboat, then lays out our lunch—tortillas with ground beef, onions, tomatoes, cheese; iced tea, frozen in plastic bags, to open and suck on—on the tailgate of the pickup truck, I stand drying slowly under this heavy noon sun. The slight nose-sting and the way the sun pulls drops from the skin give me a quick series of very clear flashes—each looking like the last but live action nonetheless—of Brigid squinting at me in her green bathing suit in the brightness, after a swim in

Piseco Lake, in upstate New York. Her hair is at its shortest, looking kind of thatched with the effects of lake water.

On the ride back to camp, I'm pogoed pleasantly, sitting alone in the back of the truck. I spot a sizable iguana on a rock; he won't look at me, but he knows I know him from Florida more than twenty years ago. Here and there is perched a stilted little home, the faces of women or children framed, motionless, in the windows. Through one I can see only the shadow of a woman rocking. Men work in the fields.

This is Mennonite land; they own great swaths of the country, supply much of its fruit and vegetables in exchange for tax breaks. They keep to themselves, and we're not allowed to photograph them, but standing there in broad hats and suspenders, with those odd, ill-fitting beards, these men look just like those we used to pass when I was a kid in Pennsylvania.

The rest of the afternoon's free, so I set off into the forest . . . SOLO. I step for half a mile down a muddy pathway behind the camp, where the horses go, and even though I know this is a laughably wimpy version of rain forest trekking, it's none other *than* the rain forest, so there's no telling what I might encounter.

Up ahead of me, off the path to the left, I can hear a strange grunting or snorting sound —peccary, tapir? My breathing catches, and I pick up a large stone, tiptoe forward. I arrive, cock the stone, and squint, bending. A bright emerald-green hummingbird flits around a bush, wings thrumming noisily. I put the stone down.

A little farther on, I hear from behind a wall of underbrush an authentic large-bodied rustling. It's getting closer, and I freeze. A minute goes by, and it's still getting closer, though patiently. Another minute. This is wonderful. It must be ninety degrees, hardly a breeze. I hold my breath, or rather, I think I'm holding my breath. And then I actually hold my breath because it's here. About fifteen feet away, on the ground, larger than a raccoon but shaped kind of like one, especially in its ringed snout and face, standing on all fours with medium-length toasty fur, its tail, though, almost black and thick and roughly two feet long, poking straight up in the air, tensile, flicking.

I guess it's a kinkajou; I heard about them at dinner last night. Farther off, three others graze calmly among green leaves. But this one is wrapped up in the question of me. I absolutely do not move, and that I don't seem to know, lately, whether I'm a creature or a mere object helps me confuse this one too; nose my way, it steps a little nearer (ten feet), emitting windy little barks, or huffs, leaning toward me, straining for a bead. We're in stand-off for two more minutes, and then I scratch my face.

The kinkajou bolts up a tree and keeps its eyes fastened on me from twelve feet off the ground, switching its sharp face from side to side of a thick intervening limb. I shout and lean into an all-out charge. The kinkajou shouts back, once, streaks the rest of the way up the tree, shrieking like a monkey, then bounds into the upper branches of the next tree, and the next, until it's gone.

King, I return to the pathway, thrust my arms up over my head, shout, "Kinkajou!"

I take a right and stride down a more rustic pathway onto land I've been told not to go far on; the owner wants it untrodden. I must insist, however, that *I* own this whole jungle now.

This path leads through brief tunnels formed by palm fronds that swirl up and over from both sides. I'm descending, not steeply but continuously. It's starting to get dusky and cooler, especially in these tunnels, and I find myself rushing to feel that specific drench of sunlight again.

After about a mile, I enter a marshy patch that could very likely host the fer-de-lance or other snakes. I was startled to learn, this morning at breakfast, that there are no antivenoms at the camp; one is simply supposed to wear rubber boots in spots like this, not the sneakers I have on.

I jog until I reach firm ground, and I'm at the head of a bright valley. Hands on hips, feet spread apart, I survey this new land and pull in mighty breaths. Gorgeous, towering cohune palms and even taller, more elaborate mimosa trees stand in a suggestion of steam rising. And, of course, a constant, intricate backdrop of birdcalls and frequent sprays of small flowers—yellow, red—showing at all different heights along the ridges on both sides.

The sun's nearly down, down here, its hard angle cutting fuzzy shapes of trees out of the celery-green valley floor.

My survey takes me eventually to my own feet, and next to my right sneaker I notice a track pressed into semisoft mud. I crouch and examine it: three-toed, big as my hand, and though I know I'm not qualified to make this judgment, it does look awfully fresh. I wish I knew puma and jaguar paws.

It suddenly seems a long, long way to my tent, and once that sun slips beneath that ridge . . .

I'm sprinting uphill (steeper than I remembered), sweat soaking my T-shirt, out through those tunnels, glancing to this side and that as vines and trunks and impenetrable clots of foliage clip past.

Back at the main building, as I'm having a strong drink before dinner, Jim tells me that it was a tapir track I saw, and that, instead of a kinkajou, my creature was a coatimundi.

• • •

After dinner, in my tent, I reunite with Brigid, feeling glad to have learned it's not so frightening or even so very complicated to visit the Castle Keep. Instead, she's *here*, that's all.

> *April 19: Juno was chewing a [rawhide] chewbie on my shins for a while, then paused and crunched peculiarly at her own mouth, and I thought, "Oh, my God, it's happening. She's eating her baby teeth." (Her chewbies have been all bloody lately.) Sure enough, she dropped something, and when I picked it up it was a few little teeth, hooked up like alabaster cabooses in a row—icch! . . .*
>
> *It's a lovely life, these days, a lot of solitude, and quietness, y' know, and no sugar (of either breed) to pass the time with. That carob rod [you sent] was quite the thing though—in both ways. HO! Just yukkin with ya Budaza.*
>
> *April 20: Hey Boodzey, I really miss yeh. It's scary living here by myself. Driving home I had terrible visions—robbery, rape, murdered pets. . . . I'm really glad for Romers, because he does keep an eye on the perimeter. . . . I'm going to bed. I'm TARRED.*
>
> *April 21: Now I'm awake again, and it's 11:14. I let Junes out, fed everybody, sat around shivering, and decided to climb back into bed. My fingers really are stiff. I'm fed up with being cold, even when I'm wearing three layers and have just had a mug of tea.*

One morning nine months later, less than a week before the accident, when it was so warm in bed and so cold everywhere else, I massaged her and tried to persuade her not to go to work, to call and tell Goddard she'd slipped and fallen in the shower. She laughed, and we decided that would be "calling in soapy foot." She *did* stay home that day and spent a lot of it lying in bed reading and napping . . . probably her all-time favorite indulgence.

xur

After a breakfast, like yesterday's, of rolls and jam and eggs and slices of watermelon and (sweetened) juice from those Jamaican oranges, I am sitting on the back of a terribly despondent horse, a peanut-colored ten-year-old male named Xur.

I and Al and Sharon and a new woman—Robin Schock, a technician at an eye bank in Hershey, Pennsylvania, who actually *scoops* them out of human skulls—set off for an eight-mile ride along the mountain trails. Chipper Aaron Beevis is in the lead, and, taking up the rear, our other guide, a Guatemalan man named Rigo, who seems shy.

Xur sighs massively between my legs, and I feel like bursting into tears. Behind me, as we begin, passing along the trail near my tent and leaving the campground, Rigo makes me nervous by clearing his throat over and over, gently and quietly, the kind of thing a person does when borderline nauseated and wishing, without admitting that there may be a problem, to stabilize the gullet.

I have not ridden a horse since I was twelve, and back then I didn't exactly *get* it. This one seems a shade too small, and even though he's plenty sturdy, the steps he takes feel labored.

We move single file onto the trail—grass and mud—and it strikes me that nothing's stirring in the forest on either side, not breeze, not even birds. And it's far too quiet. Everything just stands there, hangs there, and this same heavy, humid loaminess which has until now meant the air is laden with possibility, on the verge of quick motion or luxurious transformation that'll take me along, means today instead that the world is queasy, fetid, sullen.

But it's not until we break into a canter that I start to weep and even then it's not the good kind that others can hear. My whole torso has become a chamber for weeping; it's the sound of me sometimes, sometimes Brigid, but mostly just an anonymous weeping, and a keening, as though to represent the way any soul ought to carry on, though mine never does.

Cantering has sparked this, I think, by being so lifelike, by kicking my body into a wild plunge that would normally thrill a body, make it yell, "Aiya! Yip! Yip! Yip!" But I'm only jarred the other way, begrudging any would-be "Yip!" that might rear its happy head inside me; I'm not even "reduced to tears," I'm reduced to such a lowly place that I can't even *rise* to tears.

Not only that, but I'm constantly about to slip off and be dragged by my foot, stuck in its stirrup. After my few lessons in 1972, I knew how to "post," but that's not working here in 1994. I vise my legs onto Xur's ribs, clutch the pommel with both hands, fix my vision on Robin's red-shirted back bouncing merrily ahead, try moment by moment to rediscover the principle of balance, and emit the sort of ultra-high-pitched whine that children make when they're upset but don't want to get into trouble: "We're here on vacation to have FUN, and all you can do is COMPLAIN!"

Back to a trot, then a walk, we take a turn and begin to climb a steep, rocky hill on a narrow trail. Even here, farther inside the forest, wrapped by obscene, large-scale greenery and fulsome fragrance, as though trapped inside a madman's hothouse, nothing stirs except us in our elaborate chore. Xur struggles not to lose his footing on the mud and loose stones; he'd clearly prefer not to keep going, because he stops often and I have to kick him and say, "I know, but c'mon."

Sometimes I reach out and pat his right shoulder, lay my hand on it and feel his heat, his sweat, and the demanded swiveling of muscles. Sometimes his hooves do slip, and his head and neck plunge toward the earth until he steadies himself. Robin is getting farther ahead of us, and behind, Rigo still gently clears his throat.

I'm not the man who shouted "Kinkajou!" and ran from the tapir print; instead, I'm the sulking cave-goer feeling used again, feeling had, used and had by *myself*. Here's why self-provided adventure is infinitely sad rather than merely poignant: The effort of doing all this for myself collapses around the very idea of "for," collapses of its own unregenerate bulk. "For" is an arrow, not a boomerang. Telling myself I deserve it begs the question. Being alone is no good, and there is something inescapably unwholesome about giving *oneself* a gift like this. No, thank me.

We finally complete the hill, travel along a ridge for two hundred yards, then start down an even steeper hill, with looser stones and wetter mud. The exquisite though reluctant care that Xur must exercise in finding his footing reminds me of the type of nightmare that comes with the flu, when I'm fevered and edging ever closer to vomiting—hopelessly tedious dreams in which I'm trying to accomplish some task that continues dividing itself endlessly into subsidiary tasks, which I intricately strain to perform. And it's this half-lost, half-responsible refinement of exertion that brings on ever new dimensions of nausea.

Ahead of me, Robin is still riding well, widening the gap between us. She told me, earlier, "The worst is definitely children; that's the only time it really bothers me. You've got to get to them within six hours of death."

"So what's the actual procedure, anyway?"

"There's this kind of little curved spoon with a notch in the end that you slip in and around to the back. The notch is where the optic nerve fits. Then you take these curved scissors and slide them in behind the spoon and snip."

"Ah."

"I like to put a hemostat in on the other side, hold the ball steady so it won't swivel around."

"Makes sense."

"Now my kids say, 'Mom, quit staring at us that way,'" Robin told me. "'Ever since you got that job, you've been looking in our eyes different.' I tell 'em, 'Oh, don't be ridiculous. I've always looked in your eyes like this.'"

After fifteen minutes of clomping along the ridge, we break out mercifully into a long, sunny valley—and lo, it is time, once again, to canter!

Well, I never do throw up or weep out loud, and poor Xur

does not collapse sprawling and give up his job, only always teeters on the brink of resignation. But my balance does improve, and by the last two canterings I must say I recognize the trappings of fun in my heart rate and my lips pulled back taut in what must be a grin.

Underneath it all, though, an infinite sadness, a reprise of the cabbage in my chest, now in new jumbo-jungle-size, and rotting with the rain forest floor's world-class defecatory dankness.

Coming here has flung me into the primal world I sought, all right, but it's as if I'm sitting at the tip of one of these great cohune palm fronds, as if it's unfurled and shows me now the earth in the palsied moment before destruction.

Well, I hate it. Furl me up again like a sigh; spin me into your stale heart and keep me there.

six

Squinting, my new occupation. I disembark at the tiny airstrip and shuffle through the powdery white sand that covers the few streets of San Pedro, near the southern tip of the island off Belize called Ambergris Cay. The sun is three times brighter here, at least, bouncing off this sand and the predictably turquoise sea. Somewhere out there is the Blue Hole.

I check in to my hotel, at the end of a street lined with gift shops, dive and snorkel shops, eateries, compact grocery stores. Unabashed, pastel-wearing, some drunk-and-hooting tourists ride by in rented golf carts.

My room is dark, cavelike, air-conditioned, takes me back to the drives to Florida. After four hundred miles in the baking station wagon, late afternoons, we'd stop at a place with a pool, change into our bathing suits, and turn suddenly into some mythical, forgotten type of creature who *shivers.*

I cross the street and walk into the warm, shallow water, squat and duck-walk until it wraps my shoulders and slippery lasagna-noodle weeds begin under my feet. Sky and ocean are desperately wide open beyond and above me, so I concentrate instead on three local kids—two girls and a boy—splashing by the beach and, out here by me, a tall, brown pair of pelicans standing atop two log pillars. Well, either I'm insane or they're every bit as sad as old Xur, lawn-ornament-still, famous overlarge bills sagged down beside their throats. Spooning my own lower jaw along through the water, collecting some, then spouting it back out, I remember that tomorrow morning I have to actually *dive,* and probably *deep,* at *sea.*

Who am I fooling? I cannot forget that I never really learned to swim as a child, that therefore, at the beginning of my scuba course, I failed my endurance swimming test—breaststroke, sidestroke, backstroke—and that then at the end, after I'd practiced on my own all week, the instructor canceled my makeup test and gave me clemency because it was cold and drizzly outside and the pool had its plastic cover on.

Maybe I should just paddle around the whole four days, here by these no-pressure pelicans.

Back on the main street—Barrier Reef Drive—I pop into Out Island Divers, the shop running the Blue Hole trip, forty-eight hours from now, for which I've prepaid. I immediately learn two disturbing things from a sweet-faced young woman, Alicia, lighter-skinned and one of those uncommon possessors of an eye whose pupil has broken through its clean boundary and sent a minuscule black spit—widening into another tiny circle at its end—out into the surrounding blue of iris.

1. No, once you get to the Hole, there is no beginner's version of the dive; the whole group goes all the way down together, in just four minutes, spends eight minutes beneath the overhang,

among the giant stalactites, with flashlights, at *one hundred and thirty* feet, before ascending; it's all or nothing, and I remember the chart of "dive site ratings" for the Lighthouse Reef locations, how the Blue Hole alone takes up the most advanced category.

2. The trip may be canceled anyway because I'm the only one currently signed up for that day.

I thank Alicia and step back out onto the shiny half of the planet Mercury, feeling a nauseating mixture of relief—out of my hands, trip canceled!—and stony obligation, having come this far on a mission to face the powerful unknown, to *go down in there no matter what.*

On the phone in my hotel's office, astonishingly, I reach Joy! A more restorative ten minutes could never be. There's a dead hitch in the line every time I stop talking, before her voice comes back, but when it does it's so fresh and excited and curious about me. I rattle on, tell her that this traveling alone is *not for me,* and she promises not to let me go without her next time. I love this woman!

Veins zipping again with the right blood ("Kinkajou!"), I buy two chicken burritos and a cold can of apple juice, sit on some bleachers in a new breeze, and watch a group of boys playing basketball on the concrete court. Yum! The adventurer is back! Still hungry, I buy a strawberry ice cream cone and lick it away while stepping the whole length of San Pedro. I notice that tonight there is going to be live music by a man called Barefoot Gibby at the Purple Parrot Courtyard. All right then, I will take myself out this evening!

At the end of a longish pier, in a cute little hut, again palm-thatched, loaded with fancy, colorful scuba equipment, I introduce myself to Chango Pas, owner and principal dive master of the Amigo Dive Shop, which is the hut itself. I have vouchers for five dives out of here, the first being tomorrow morning.

His round, chestnut-hued face and black eyes are stark; he's short, his body thick and cured by decades of water pressure. He's cordial, but those eyes of his seem to slander me somehow; he scares me, I guess, only because drowning does. "Not a problem," Chango tells me. "Be here at a quarter to nine."

Nighttime, still seventy-five degrees. I've had a shower and a nap and sit now on the roofed patio of Mary Ellen's Little Italy, slowly eating a plate of spaghetti with red snapper sauce and a whole loaf of soft, warm bread, and drinking a bottle of Belikin beer. Over the ocean, the moon is finally full, and it lays down one of those shimmering, romantic pathways leading right this way, but I have to crane to see it because a post blocks my view.

All around me, of course, couples eat, sip wine, chatter, don't need to crane. Brigid's sitting across from me at our small table, smiling and smiling, sort of like the Cheshire cat, as I tell her— whispering—about some of the things that have been happening to me. And closer, at my right hand, sits Joy—solider, green-eyed, black-haired, sexy, patient.

Barefoot Gibby is barefoot indeed, fat, an American, belting out a particularly unctuous version of "Dream Lover" to a crowd of about seven of us. When he's done, he says, "Hey, we'll be partyin' here at the Purple Parrot till about midnight. If ya have any requests, hey, let me know, and if not, well *hey,* that's okay too."

The first line of his next number is, "If I toldja ya had a beautiful body, wouldja hold it against me?"

Back in my room, I take out the nightshirt Brigid usually wore to bed; it's long (almost to her knees), green-navy-yellow-red plaid, 100 percent cotton, with a small rip just under the right arm. I crawl into bed naked and wrap it around me (mmmmmmm rather than spooky), ready to have a full-fledged dream about her at last.

Instead, it's about Joy. She's given birth to two babies, whom she's neatly packaged in brown paper. When she opens them, one is dead and the other is perky. The perky one she starts to nurse, and her chest is hers except for the fact that it's covered with *my* chest hair. I ask her how it feels to nurse, and she says, matter-of-factly, "Good."

At ten after seven, it's already blinding outside my window, so I keep the heavy drapes shut and lie here gently gripping the nightshirt, afraid to dive but also, startlingly, shaking with excitement—it's another *world* down there!

Keep me company, though?

Brigid's sixth letter from our time apart is five pages long, single-spaced on our old Panasonic printer. I switch on my fluorescent bed light and begin reading.

swedish meatballs, pepper steak, and my pea-green partner

Bambino says, "Okay. We go to the bottom right here, forty-five feet, then we go over the edge into the canyon, to sixty feet, seventy feet. At one place we might go through a tunnel."

Bambino is Chango's brother, with the same eyes. We're two miles out to sea, bobbing in a small white and blue motorboat. Here, beyond the coral reef, the water's dark, heavy gray, not pretty turquoise anymore. I'm strapped into my suit, heavy tank on my back. The other two divers are Bill, who certified in the late sixties, and a bearded Frenchman actually named Monsieur Chevalier.

"We all ready?"

"Um, I just have to tell you one thing," I force myself to confess. "I'm a real beginner, and I don't know—"

"Is not a problem," says Bambino. "You stick with me. Okay, let's go."

He and the others topple over backward from the side of the boat, one by one, and then so do I, a horrible crash. Though I don't have to tread water because I've inflated my BC (buoyancy compensator, the vest you wear that takes on air through a tube from your tank with the press of a button), I'm flailing and on the verge of panic right away; swells keep rushing at me and slapping my face, making me sputter; I failed my endurance swimming test; and I'm supposed to go so unbearably far down, to the bottom and into a canyon, a tunnel!

Bill and Monsieur Chevalier have disappeared below already, and Bambino and I are staring rather intimately into each other's eyes through our face masks. He's trying to will me to relax.

"I don't know, I don't know if I'm ready."

"You jus' hyperventilating. You gotta calm down. Put yer face in and look at the bottom. Keep yer eyes on the bottom; don't look at the surface. Jus' follow me."

He paddles closer, and it's only now that I see for the first time a long, white staff in his hand; it's hooked at the end, and I get the distinct impression that he plans to snag my BC and yank me under.

"No!"

Bambino shoves me back toward the boat in obvious disgust and sinks out of sight. I'm nearly back safely to the ladder when the younger dive shop guy, who has to stay with the boat, leans over and says, "If you want you can go down by the rope back there, to the anchor." He is taking marvelous pity on me, because really it's against the rules for them to send a diver down by himself; it's much more dangerous than the group dive I just refused. "You can go as slow as you want."

"Thank you, thanks a lot."

And I *do* use the rope, thick and solid in my hands, let the air out of my BC and then angle downward through water chillier than yesterday's shallows. Hand over hand, length by ginger length, I pull myself toward an anchor lost at the bottom, a bottom which, I see, is scattered all over with promising locations —boulders and little caves and fan coral and spheres of perfectly named brain coral lying beside straight alleyways of sand—and whose distance beneath me is now suddenly a draw more than a fright.

It takes whole minutes to equalize, or "clear" my ears. During the first thirty-three feet of descent, the pressure on the body doubles, but this only poses a problem for air spaces: lungs, sinuses, behind the eardrums. The regulator you breathe through adjusts the pressure of the air to match that of the surrounding water at your current depth, which works fine for the lungs and (unless you have a cold) the sinuses, but until your eustachian tubes are clear, the air behind your eardrums will remain at the former pressure, and the difference causes intense pain and can pop your eardrums if you don't heed the pain before it gets too bad, stop and equalize the pressure by clamping your nose shut and gently blowing to clear those tubes and let the new-style air flow up and relieve you.

I reach bottom and hang just above some rocks. It's gloomy down here, except that lots of tiny bright blue and yellow neon fish flit around—like fireflies at dusk, but always *on*—as well as much larger grunts—standard fish-shape but with striking canary-yellow stripes and tails—hurrying on errands singly and in pairs. My gauge reads forty feet, the deepest I've ever been, and I'm very proud of myself, though also more than a little unnerved, all alone in this silence broken only by the amplified noise of my throat sucking life through a slender tube, spitting it back out as bubbles, as though ungrateful, then greedily sucking more.

With my eyes, I follow the good old rope back up, far, to where the boat's hull swishes like a toy's at the choppy surface. I revolve, checking in all directions, and although it's nice to be able to see for thirty feet in every direction, this doesn't take away from the opaque, greenish murk of the periphery. Every now and then, real anxiety starts to rise, I get addled, and to fight this I fix my mind on parts of the letter I just read in bed.

It was raining like a rain machine on a Hollywood set when I got home . . . so I took Junes for a long walk through town, and . . . we hung out under the marquee at the Caps [Capital Theater] until a boy came in his neon biker togs, and stared at Juno anxiously at first, and then more fondly, until he tapped at her tentatively. . . . [She started] straining at the boy, and then burrowing her head into my skirt and whining, wanting to go, and kissing me, and wiggling and looking around; you could see her taking on character for this kid. Then we just walked right into the downpour because she asked me would I, and we walked down Langdon Street, over the bridge (Junes stuck her nose through the bridge . . . very charmingly, curious about what-was-this-river?) . . . and a girl was standing in the doorway of Onion River Sports with a leaking bag of popcorn letting little kernels drop onto the wet pavement as she craned her neck over her shoulder, back into the store to someone . . .

Lying still on sand among rocks and waving fan coral, there's a moray eel. I sink in for a better look, and his color can only be described as electric pea green. He points his beaky mouth up at me and bites the water, but he's only about three feet long, and the stone walls touching both sides of him convince me he can't turn quickly if I do this . . . run the fingers of my right hand along his back. His skin is smooth and scaleless, the flesh very firm, and he only jerks ahead slightly, not going anywhere. I'll be coming back to you, partner, but first I swim over and down into the nearest of those alleyways of sand—which turn out to be modest valleys—and begin traveling along it slowly, at forty-seven feet, mask just inches from tiny, transparent darters, thousands of pale shell fragments (the layer of the eventual fossil record that means, generally, "today"), hefty crabs escaping left and right into exact-fit pockets under stones, and scuttling hermit crabs in shells the size of dud popcorn kernels.

I keep glancing up and back over my tank and shoulder to make sure the rope is still in view; sometimes I have to rise over short walls of those brain corals; sometimes I pause to trace along their crazy grooves with my index finger.

> *[Later, I walked Romers] down the tracks and around the depot . . . good as gold, because the tracks and the rusting flatcar beds (or whatever they're called—there's one very poignant one just behind our house which, amid all the rust, has the words* DEDICATED SERVICE *still on it) and empty boxcars and weeds, and the trash on the river bank are all so sad and real in the rain . . . and I thought for the first time in a long while about the romance of Montpelier.*

I'm cold and miss my rope, so I swim quickly back, visit my eel, whose very tiltable black, gold-flecked eyes pursue my every move and whose cute-fanged mouth opens and shuts toward my face: "You are no partner of mine."

I slide to where the anchor lies on its side half buried in mud, grab the rope, and start up, watching this now familiar place fall away from me forever. I climb with exaggerated prudence, so my lungs won't rupture. The rule is, do not exceed the speed of your slowest bubble.

I have eaten two Budget Gourmets, and I realized that they are, in fact, quite the most pathetic freezer entrees I have ever eaten; you slash the tops with a knife, cook for a half-hour, rip this cardboard husk off, and then stir. *The components lurking there may vary, but you must ever stir, because they are frozen cheek by jowl, the Swedish meatballs and the noodles, the pepper steak and the rice, and to leave them unstirred is out of the question, the one being so very gluey, the other so desiccated. They* need *each other, like you and I, and* must *be mixed before ingestion.*

I'm back in the boat and free of BC and tank and mask just five minutes before Bill and Monsieur Chevalier and Bambino show up and come aboard. I was down "for a half-hour." On the way back to San Pedro, although I am feeling quite triumphant, Bambino's still angry with me. Twice he holds up his white staff, tells me it's for pointing at *fish,* not for pulling people *down,* and he gets us all to laugh by shaking his head at me, rolling his eyes, shouting into the wind, "He jus' needs be . . ." and making a broad, vigorous spanking motion with his free hand.

I have done my best to charm you . . . and I hope you have some respect for a hardworking girl. I am enjoying right now the feeling that you will love me with your whole heart when you're done reading this letter.

sprize!

Sick of fighting this current that wants to carry me through the notch, into the riptide, and out to sea, I reach out and grab a plant. Immediately, my hand and forearm begin burning, because this is fire coral, like nettles. Diego turns and motions me not to touch, shaking his head sternly. I disappoint them all. Then he resumes his relaxed floating with the current, his hands folded prayerfully in front of his belly. I scratch my burned arm and kick hard to keep up with him.

It's two-thirty in the afternoon, and we're twenty feet down inside the Hol Chan Marine Reserve, protected by the reef. Everywhere are big, beautiful fish in shafts of sunlight. But before we dove in, Diego pointed to a notch in the reef wall, maybe fifty yards from our boat, in the direction we are now swimming, and said, "The current goes that way, and out there is a tide."

"Rip?" I said.

"Yah."

In other words, it's a funnel. He expects me to trust his years of experience, to drift with him across and with the current, kicking lazily every now and then, toward the notch but not too close, across the broad valley that leads to it and into calmer going on the other side. And really, the flow's never stronger than I, but I might wear out, and I'm not pleased to be plunged into this slow-motion crisis, and caustic salt water has trickled into my eyes, and of course I cannot wipe them. All the while, Diego's chestnut hands stay laced together in front of him. Eventually, trying to breathe smoothly and deeply, I put mine together too.

Except, here and there, in our progress through this broad valley—bounded on both sides by tall hills of rock and soft, swaying, weedlike coral—he unfolds his, I mine, and draws my attention. Large, sad-clown groupers hover near, each alone, gray. A manta ray flaps up from out of the sand and moves off to where it's darker. A pair of toothy barracudas hang thirty feet away, motionless, like objects in a mobile where there's no breeze.

Diego picks up by one foot a creature looking for all the world like a daddy longlegs spider, only each of his six legs is longer than my hand, and his body is pointy-snouted instead of spherical. I take his foot from Diego and hold it between index and first fingers; he kicks to get loose, and I laugh with bubbles at how unlikely he is, then I let him go.

I hesitate before the wide mouth of a dark cave, but then, peering through to see light at the other end just ten feet away, I follow my dive master in. Claustrophobia begins to hot-spice my spine, but it's cooled right away by our exiting. As soon as we do, I'm shocked by the sight, off to my right: a bank of silver fish shaped like tuna but each maybe a foot or two long, hundreds of them knit together into a chinkless surface, rising to fifteen feet above me, utterly still and bright as new metal in the angling sunlight. My salted eyes sting more. It's the most gorgeous and alarming thing I've seen underwater, their suddenness and solidarity, the way the silence both belies and ups the drama; my mind supplies that suspense-movie string-section encounter-halt: choooongggg! For a beat, I'm just flinched, humble, happy, all my shadows found and flashed away.

This is new. I can. I *can*! Taken back, sometime in warm weather, late the summer before the accident, or early that fall?

I'm here on my bed at the Barrier Reef Hotel, evening, masturbating, and I *can be with her like this* for the first time. All these months, I could manage nothing more than chilly blips of fantasy.

I don't know. After reading a few more letters—sprize!—I fell easily into this, reliving an event.

Still light outside the bedroom windows, in Montpelier. Rare, rare, today Brigid's been let inside our lovemaking, and I'm rejoicing. On top of me, she moves without inhibition, chasing down orgasm. So natural and yet, for her, so unnatural, to be in her body like this, that I can only press with one hand on her lower back and praise whatever's allowing this to be, pull her to me again and again with my other arm around her shoulders. Just before she comes, a lightest hint of perspiration, preslippery, sweet-envelopes her skin.

It's finally true springtime, one afternoon in April, and she leaves Goddard to take a walk in the woods with a friend; work has

been draining her all winter, leaving her nothing with which to
write fiction.

> *I stood by a rushing river and threw my head back and said,*
> *"WAH!" I also said, "Oh! look! I'm in the world! I'm in it! Look!*
> *Look!" On the way [back] to Montpelier, I said, "I'm being robbed,*
> *robbed!" That about sums up my feelings.*—from letter number 10

She lies on her stomach, then, I on her back, and we fuse like
we always hope to, like I have fantasized about, as has she. We
are Caitlin and Dylan, finally, in Belize, and I'm out to squeeze
my "flesh into [hers], to mangle [her] with my strong bones,
mingle, mutilate the two of us together."

The first moment after I have come, she starts laughing, saying, "Oh, my God, oh my God, I can't believe it! I totally spaced
out on the diaphragm. I can't believe it! That's *so unlike* me! Oh,
my God." I laugh with her. We say, "Geeez." But later, maybe
it was days later, we both quietly admit that it was wonderful
having had nothing between us. I think I suggested she may have
unconsciously meant to forget, and she, I think, said maybe.

Lying here quietly now in my dark room, I find I'm able to
take a low-key, all-the-time-in-the-world survey of her body,
every little moment of it, given so vividly back. I never expected
this. Such a relief. To see, once again, the exact liver-colored
freckles strewn across her shoulders and upper back, to run fingers over them and reconfirm, as so often, that though they may
appear to float off her otherwise chalk-white skin, they are in fact
part of it; to rub her neck, her toes, slowly the muscles of her
notorious legs, in all the ways I would and will; to get a look at
her real face, all photographs aside, from an inch away, what a

grant: that slight fuzz on her upper lip, the coarse, red-brown eyebrows, the closed lids (I assume she is asleep) even whiter than chalk, with tiny blue veins in them, the eighth-of-a-circle curve of lashes. I go on and on. Nowhere is off-limits.

Then I pull her nightshirt to me again and this time focus only on the cuffs, smelling them (certain that some cells haven't been successfully washed away), nipping at them, pinching, feeling *this,* the very place her wrists go, then feeling her wrists themselves, with startling precision, the delicacy of their bones, how comically weak they get when I grab them and she pretends I can bend them any whichway at will. I have her hands too now, her own body-favorite. Her slim fingers excelled at being fingers. I rub her whole hands, carefully out the length of each of these fingers, which I happen to know feels incredibly good.

(For weeks after the accident, a recurring thought was, All night, maybe I can believe *she* has died, but her *hands?*)

How funny. Far better than all this Big Experience I've been after—the Beast! . . . the Risk!—touching these cuffs does the trick, calls up my blood, my lava, hastens to restore life.

I don't care anymore if the Blue Hole trip *is* canceled.

Facing Danger, I've discovered, leaves me very timid, shrunken, chastened. Is it too direct, generic, issuing the wrong sort of challenge?

But this smallness here—it has me rising and filling to meet it.

Y ou shood note do enay-ting you do
        note fel come-for-tabel with," says
        Monsieur Chevalier, whose brown
beard looks kind this morning, his eyes neutral as fishes'. "Moost aksidawnce ahpen to
beegeenairs."

We're back at the Amigo Dive Shop, and
the moment has come for me to decide
whether or not to get on the boat. I pried
myself out of the good, engulfing dimness of
my room ten minutes ago and dragged my
duffel bag full of equipment down the street
and to the end of this pier. I asked Chango
what kind of dive was planned. He said, rap-
idly, some site name, and sixty or seventy feet,
and when I said, "Well, y'know, I might just
go underneath the boat, on the rope, like I
did yesterday," his face turned sour. "Ah no,
we do not like for people to do that. It is not
safe."

Ever since, I've been pacing this short
room, staring at underwater pictures on the
walls. Chango has twice asked all those who
are going to get their BCs and regulators on-
board. I'm not sure, but I think Bambino's

running the show again. Chango seems like he wants to slap me; his brother must have warned him.

"Der was dis ghee in Frawnce, was down joost fifteen meatairs . . . mmm, forty-five feet . . . poor ghee . . . ee paneek and SHOOT to dee serfas, and eez loongs . . . POW!"

If a person may fairly be said to *trudge* through blaring sunshine and sand like talc, that's what I do, defeated, back down the pier and to my coward's room; I sit hunched on the bed.

Didn't last night teach me to separate self-esteem from bravery? Stop measuring everything by whether it pleases Chango and his brother!

I bolt out the door, through town, and onto the one narrow blond-dusty road leading south, past concrete construction sites, men pouring foundations, carefully laying bricks to form a wall, operating dozers, clearing earth. I take off my T-shirt, tie it around my waist, and start to jog, and pretty soon there are palms and ferns on both sides, pathways leading off to sunny clearings. Only here and there, a low wooden home.

I'm breathing round*er,* though not quite *round.* The heat insists, through my bare back, that I'm worthy. I feel almost empty, but I ate several little bananas and drank apple juice this morning to prepare for the ocean floor, so this emptiness doesn't gnaw.

To my left I spot an iguana, halfway up a palm with tall trunk and crown on top, unlike the cohunes out west. I stop jogging and step toward the magnificent lizard; including tail he must be eighteen inches long. Claws on bark sound amplified as he scampers around to the other side and peeks out, as squirrels have so often done with me. I edge my face toward him, and he retreats a step. We're breathing the same air. I go on my way, running faster, breathing even better, and that sun's got a spotlight on my smile. "Oh! look! I'm *in* the *world*! I'm in it! Look! Look!"

I will learn today whether the Blue Hole is off, and if so I will get my money back and use that money to buy what I saw advertised in town, a flight to the mainland, then a trip into the jungle on a riverboat, in the northeast part of the country. These last few days' adventure I'll simply shift from sea to land. I will take that cruise, and then I'll drive my rental car, already booked, back west and much deeper into the jungle than I went before —before was for babies!—no matter how bad the roads are. Oh, and they'll be bad. I might have to abandon the vehicle in a crater and run through the forest. I'll be hell-bent for monkeys, for snakes, toucans, tapirs, peccaries, maybe even for the mighty jaguar! Like to see stocky Chango go where I'll be going, run like me!

I arrive at an abandoned project off to my right—just a glum cement-and-wood frame for a two-story structure—beside a large, stagnant pond. I stand on the bank. My legs are humming. Down through an oily surface film I can see dark fish move. I pick up a dried green coconut and arc it out a ways. The sound really *is* ker-plunk.

Out behind the work site is a field of sparse grass, stones, and occasional trees, plus, I'm charmed to find, hanging from a thick bough, a swing, two clean yellow ropes tied to either side of a long, wide board.

I sit, take the ropes in my hands, push off, lie back, and pull with my arms stretched straight. The motion through this very first back-and-forth draws something out of me like a colored handkerchief from a magician's sleeve. I'm sobbing before I know it, and the more I swing—making of myself that old, old pendulum from about the time I learned to walk—the more I can cry. Some of it sounds good, long wails like a plain megaphone from the heart, but some's that ugly hacking kind that men do, tough. It's real crying, though, not presumed, like on Xur.

"I just don't want to be so far away from you anymore!"

I say it again and again, through gritted teeth. The demands of crying—rhythms of anger and breath—cause me to stress different words each time. "I JUST don't want to be so far away from you anymore!" "I just don't WANT to be so far away from you anymore!" "I just don't want to BE so far away from you anymore!" "I just don't want to be SO far aWAY from you anyMORE!" And then I quiet down—". . . just don't want to be so far away from you . . ."—before picking up strength again.

A passage comes back to me, from Brigid's story "Sweet on Ross." It's at a point near the end, after the narrator has left her husband but kidnapped his dog, having fallen in love with him. She takes him to a park.

> I meandered over to a swingset and sat down on one of the canvas seats. My legs were immediately and involuntarily crossed by the pressure the seat exerted: clearly my backside had grown too broad for the playground.
>
> With difficulty, and despite a wide puddle, I pushed myself off using my lower foot, and soon I was swinging into the tree

branches before me. I gulped in great draughts of air, and leaned back into the declining glory of my twenty-seventh summer, my hair fluttering on my head like a family of streamers. The swingset groaned and squeaked with an unfamiliar urgency, and the rusty chains writhed and popped against my palms. . . . How tired we get of life, I thought, and how hard it is to recall *what* it is. A bluejay flapped by just out of reach, and I laughed and kicked my heels about. . . . Never mind, I whispered to myself, closing my eyes: never mind. I was light, sky-bound, ripe for the future, for the long, easy days with my dog, my second soul.

I keep up my refrain, sometimes adding, "I've come all this way to look for you, you can swing in me," and "Never mind, never mind, never mind."

We swing and swing.

Why can't we swing till nightfall and dawn, till high-rise hotels sprout up all around our tree, till they crumble? Is it because my crying has stopped already, and my refrain? And is *that* because I have become pleased with myself?

Alicia—Out Island Divers shop, inkblot pupil—finalizes the Blue Hole cancellation. Yay. But the dive master, a tall American with unnervingly clear blue eyes, tries to persuade me to switch to tomorrow's "Turneffe Island" trip, whose most spectacular stop is "The Elbow," so called because it's just off the island's southernmost promontory.

Back in my room, I consult the trusty dive-site booklet: "The Elbow is considered an advanced dive because of environmental conditions. Seas are often rough even on calm days because of large ocean swells. . . . Once in the water, currents usually sweep divers out toward deep water beyond the reef. . . . Excellent buoyancy control and air consumption simply are a must."

Back at the shop, I decline the switch and receive my refund, for which I feel a bit sheepish, but better for the presence of a tall and gentle American woman, about my age, who gives me a few sympathetic words, doesn't blame me for fearing death. I take that money to a travel agency and spend most of it on the tickets for tomorrow's jungle cruise.

After eating some more little bananas, swigging more apple juice, I present myself once again to Chango Pas. As soon as he sees me, he says, kind of coyly, "Hello, señor," and together we laugh the we-both-know-I'm-a-big-baby laugh, cutting the considerable tension that has become a part of our relationship. It turns out this shop is running a trip this afternoon to a place called Mexico Rocks, twelve feet deep, zero current. It's really for snorkelers, but, says Chango, "You can jus play around in dare, okay?" Okay!

It's a perfect final dive, fifty-five uninterrupted minutes upon broad, sunny fields of bright sand, with here and there an oasis, a dark green mound (six or eight feet high) of stones and hard coral, soft coral waving too, common home to an immensely gladdening jumble of fish. I've got neutral buoyancy, precisely balanced between rising and sinking, so that I can swim along inches above the sand, breathing shallow, and then, since air in the lungs is lighter than air in the tank, I can, as I approach an oasis, merely by drawing a deep breath, climb automatically, glide over the top, noting as many as possible of the pockets of coiled color and tiny interactive dramas passing beneath me, before exhaling, which drops me gently back to sand-level again on the other side. Haven't had such a flying-dream in maybe fifteen years. "Oh! Look! Look!"

I take pictures with a rented underwater camera: creamy yellow bottom feeders as they trowel through the finest top layer, lifting clouds; a shadowy, prodigious fellow who stays always twenty feet off, seems as long as my arm; and midsized, slate-shaded guys I call cruisers, who make me laugh, because they'll emerge from one side of the circle of visibility and motor, in ones and twos, right past me, utterly on course and perfectly uninterested in me, and disappear out the other side, gone forever. I happen simply to be stationed here off their straight highway, witnessing a segment maybe one-thousandth its full length.

Also, I sit still before small caves at the base of oases, snap angelfish, indigo and scarlet and powder blue and orange and purple; incandescent minnow-sizers in all these hues and more; lots of those lemon-striped grunts from my first dive; and the squirrelfish, cardinal red with their distinctively spiny top fin, like overlapping plates that make a razor-sharp sheet of armor. If I hold out my hand, all these fish—except of course the cruisers—come sniff and even tap the tips of my fingers.

At several moments, a current of pure electricity is released, paralyzing me with gratefulness-to-be-exactly-here, and once, it screams out of me in a hail of bubbles.

Back in San Pedro, night's here, and the quietly triumphant reach-and-grab of round-breathing visits me every twentieth breath or so.

"Now let's eat ourselves into a dandy swivet."

I buy a huge pizza with sweet peppers, pineapple, and sausage, carry it and two bottles of Belikin back to my room, eat and drink my farewell dinner to diving. A toast: now, finally, I've known you on equal terms; I'll be able to fantasize about you in the future, an intimate.

It turns out the tall American woman from the dive shop is on the jungle cruise with me; her name is Adrian, and we hang around together all day. It further turns out that—*even though she's not an advanced diver*—she is braving the Blue Hole *tomorrow,* when the trip is rescheduled for; I'll be headed back to the mainland, to pick up my four-wheel-drive Suzuki Samurai, hell-bent, of course, for monkeys.

On the boat ride up the New River, with ten other tourists and our guide, Mario, we see a young three-foot crocodile, bats hanging asleep in a tree, and lots of high-stepping, long-legged birds.

We dock by the ancient Mayan site called Lamanai, believed to have been built and occupied in 1500 B.C. Ninety degrees and humid. Shady, classically jungly pathways leading to giant stone heads, elaborate carvings, and pyramids over a hundred feet tall that we raise our arms on top of. On the back side of one of these, we come across a boa constrictor twined around thick roots. It's only a four-footer; I stroke the vividly painted skin.

High in another tree, there's a black toucan, with a lime-green bill, and in another, a troupe of, yes yes, *howler monkeys,* relaxing, napping. It's hard to see them from so far below, but one clearly cares for a floppy infant.

Though it seems obvious that we are not going to fall in love, Adrian is excellent company; she has that relaxing type of long, thin face that doesn't seem to know how to forget a person.

And by the time she takes a picture of me standing beside the pocked stone head, taller than me, I've already made my decision: These animals, this heat, these great, broad leaves slapping into my face as I walk, all represent what I was hoping to find only out west. And when I tell Adrian what I'm thinking now, she says she'll be happy to be my dive buddy.

I'm amazed, but I've found I'm suddenly unwilling to have traveled so far, with the Blue Hole hanging patient in my mind's eye, only to squander this second chance. And now the point isn't to face the Dark Unknown for its Danger (indeed, it was by *releasing* that goal, at the dive shop, that I met Adrian and put myself in position for this better choice) but rather to explore it out of sheer living curiosity.

Tonight, having called Budget Rent A Car and explained, having signed up for the trip and agreed to be at the dock at 5:15 in the morning, I lie here trying to picture myself sinking into the Hole. Nobody knows I'll be there, not a soul, because, after the first trip was canceled, I called my mother to relieve her, and she's certainly told everyone else. And I'm not going to be so callous as to call her back now. One hundred and thirty feet down into cold, inky blackness collapsing over me. Like the descent into a mineshaft. It's insane. I'm a rank beginner, only been on four dives, hardly one-third as deep. These people should be arrested for even taking my money. I have absolutely no earthly idea whether I will panic, seize up, be in big trouble. Maybe Adrian will let me hold her hand.

One hundred and thirty feet . . . well, okay, that's just thirteen basketball hoops in height, only forty-three yards, less than half a football field, a hefty breakaway run.

But straight down. Into the dark, and then under a ceiling of rock. Go up and you'll bang your head. Most nightmares aren't nearly this bad. And it's *me*, the feeble one who failed his endurance swimming test.

In what is probably my favorite picture of her, Brigid's in a silly pose, like the "little teapot" from the song, wearing her forest-green and red striped turtleneck shirt. I've brought that shirt along, and now I take it out of its plastic bag and examine it. Seems not to have faded at all. Maybe it hasn't been washed since. It says her so loudly.

I take off my T-shirt, put this on. Feels good, not much too small. Except the collar is higher than I suspected, scuffing against my sunburned neck. In the photograph, she has it folded over in half. I do the same, carefully, so it's neat, but first I let it ride up over the bottom of my face, smell and bite the fabric, rub my lips against it like a horse's against a palm.

In the morning I will be going down in a small group of divers, but completely alone in that nobody will stand between me and the possibility of panic.

I didn't bring the picture of Brigid with me—or any picture —but I look at it anyway. I'm frightened, and I hug the shirt to my body. Of course I can't get it tight enough.

Hugging Brigid never felt close enough, either. We said we wished we could climb into each other's chests.

Walking through San Pedro before dawn, bag of equipment in hand, I watch sand blowing from right to left across Barrier Reef Drive. A small brown dog crosses too, way ahead. The warmth of the air—I'm starting to sweat—doesn't go with its dimness. The moon is midway between horizon and top of sky, and it's just a little larger than half. But it was *full* only a few *nights* ago, as I sat on the patio of Mary Ellen's Little Italy. Why is it waning so fast? Far out at sea, to my left, I can hear a steady, hollow roar, like a wind coming from the direction of sunrise, or what will *be* sunrise, pinkening the clouds already but still, I guess, an hour away.

I step along the wood of the dock, which gives a little, and into the twenty-foot boat, sit down heavily on a long, cushioned bench. There are four people here, an older couple, whose names I don't ask because I'm trembling, and a couple in their forties, from Vancouver, who introduce themselves as Rory and Katya. Soon, the dive master, Juan, in his early thirties, hair still puffy from the pillow, jumps aboard and asks how many more we're expecting. "Two, I think," I say, "one of whom is Adrian, whom I met yesterday." This overly formal use of two *whoms* in one short sentence chagrins me, causes me to tremble even more.

Juan's younger assistant appears on the higher level, up front, where the steering wheel is, though I didn't see him climb aboard. Adrian arrives, sleepy, glad to see I've made it, and then Gordon, thirties, from Australia. Kicking up and inhaling a great plume of sour exhaust, we push away from the dock, putter for ten minutes, stop at Cay Caulker to pick up a young Italian guy, who seems to be in his twenties, and then we're off for real, into open water.

Along the horizon a few thunderheads are massed. But above them, to my right, the moon reminds me of the Tuesday night, the first night after the morning's crash, and several hours after death, when I looked at the three-quarter moon, eyeball-insultingly stark, through the upstairs bedroom window, and said to my mother, beside me, "I *just* don't know where she *is.*"

Everyone's extremely friendly, but it's too loud for small talk, so since there's plenty of room I lie down on the cushioned bench, stare—literally—into space, steely through sparse cloud cover. I'm worried about getting seasick, even though it's a relatively calm day. The bouncing and tossing registers in my gut, and I'm not so sure I can withstand it.

Before too long, the sun comes up, and I'm feeling better, locked onto palest blue. Coasting, lulled, I pass the first of the three hours.

I breathe deep (not round) and try to let go of it all. In fact, looking up into infinity like this, I try to dissolve the nut-to-crack that is my brain, to relinquish this whole precious, tedious project of figuring out Brigid's ending and my continuing. I imagine myself drawn up and absorbed into this blue, as I will soon be into the Hole, and I try to want it, to gather myself and release myself at once. I'm just one measly pinprick of consciousness, after all.

This "after all" reminds me of a mental device I used to use to shrink what had happened. I titled this device "She is, after all, a me," and it goes like this: If *I* were faced with my death, I would be *disappointed,* would think, So there go all I'd hoped to *do,* to *know,* to *have,* to *feel,* but this would not amount to the limitless cosmic crime that Brigid's death seems from the outside. *Inside* herself, even at death, she is ordinary, finite, "just me," and disappointed, yes, bitterly, bitterly, but only disappointed.

I'm fed up with this futile fever dream of nonstop spoiling for insights, sweeping, redeeming ones. It's a trap, one that has seemed far too large but is in truth much too small. It's become a self-provoking enterprise, these delicate tricks of thought always under way, millions of them, like I'm working a combination lock—unrepeatable nuances, more refined than anything I've been able to say in this book, too complicated to be recalled even a moment later—a lock in the sleet-colored door of a safe, tumblers tumbling, until that sound of falling into place, remote and intimate, then the swinging open. And then?

No, it's closed, *and* empty, and too small, and doing all this has been required just in order for me to keep *deserving* her.

Now the Blue Hole, there's something big enough to move around inside. Let me out, into it. Let my water landing come *true* at last, the sinking away from the world. It's better than metaphors—though that's heretical for a writer to say—because they're how my mind has chewed itself up. At one thousand feet across and almost five hundred feet deep, the Hole is bigger than the world, because the world isn't the world anymore; it's "the world," is "being alive," is "being dead," merely a Gordian knot, mere because so cunningly, coyly wound.

> How tired we get of life, I thought, and how hard it is to recall *what* it is. . . . Never mind, I whispered to myself, closing my eyes: never mind.

I decline the breakfast of sweet buns, juice, and coffee. Still on my back, staring faithfully up, past clouds and obsolete fear, I'm yawned graciously into the sky. I say it over and over and over. "Never mind, never mind, never mind." I close my eyes: "Never mind."

Less than an hour from the Hole, Juan hands around a pink laminated sheet of paper describing the dive.

First, there's a sandy slope that falls off at a forty-five-degree angle to a depth of fifty-five feet, then a vertical stone wall that drops from there to one hundred and ten feet, where there's that stone ceiling from which hang stalactites stretching to a depth of one hundred and thirty-five feet.

If a diver cannot equalize his ears and get down to the stalactites within four minutes, he must give up immediately and return to the surface.

We will spend only eight minutes at maximum depth, because at this pressure nitrogen builds up in the system; approximately 15 percent of divers experience "rapture of the deep" (or nitrogen narcosis), a mild but disorienting buzz. (I remember how my instructor back in Northampton told us that divers have been known, under nitrogen narcosis, to see that fish are managing to live without regulators in their mouths and to believe that *they too* can do without them.)

After eight minutes, we'll begin our slow ascent.

I can tell we're getting close when Juan cuts the engines way down, aiming us between buoys that mark the dangerous near-surface outcroppings of Lighthouse Reef. It's time to suit up, and I stand, shakily, go through the routine slowly, slowly. Attach tank to BC, hook up all tubes, put on weight belt, sit and fit arms through BC straps, pull straps tight, Velcro its cummerbund snug over belly. Mask and flippers aren't till right before jumping in.

Gordon and Rory and the Italian boy seem lighthearted, rugged, ready for anything, fine male specimens, guys well accustomed to seizing life by the tusks. They joke around with one another about things not related to this dive, things I don't quite catch. I laugh too, act natural. Adrian doesn't look that worried, traitor. It's okay, though, because I know I'm alone anyway. She asks how I'm feeling, and I answer, "Not so bad."

The older couple and Katya are just going to snorkel above the reef that surrounds the Hole, in fifteen feet of water. Everybody seems kind, creepily kind, which makes it easy for me to envision, again and again, exactly how my not coming up alive will register on their faces, stricken as only the kind can be, in their various seats, couples holding each other, Adrian's long-thin dismay, Juan's indicted record, all staring into space, eyes ticking—the interminable ride back to San Pedro.

Juan hops down, beamish, from the upper deck, throws the

anchor in. We're here, poised on top of the Rim Itself, which is just a vague boundary of lightish reef bending out in front of us. The Hole must be beneath that calm surface, right *there*, although from this angle the water sure looks the same color as the rest of the ocean.

As he suits himself up, Juan explains that he's done this dive five hundred times, and only recently did he have his first emergency. "A girl panicked and shot up to the surface from one hundred ten feet," he says. "Don't do that."

I remember Monsieur Chevalier's story about the "ghee" whose lungs went *"pow!"* and the paragraph in the scuba textbook about rising too quickly, about "the bends," about nitrogen bubbles forming, traveling to the brain, and embolizing before you can be rushed to a recompression chamber. This can occur no matter whom you're diving with; they neglect you for an instant and good-bye.

Juan says that there's no marine life down there, "except killer sharks. They need to eat three tourists every week." We laugh, extra hard. This is not going to be so bad. Walking around the deck in the sun, listening to Juan and the others in high spirits, and to the water patting, like water anywhere, at the sides of our hull, I'm finding it difficult to keep my grimface on, even secretly underneath my acting-natural face.

But when we step off the platform at the back of the boat and, one by one, enter the water flippers first, when we inflate our BCs and start kicking, on our backs, at our own rates of speed, across the Hole to that reef where Juan's told us there's going to be an orange buoy, four hundred feet from the boat, where we'll regroup and get ready to let the air *out* of our BCs, well that's when there go skittering across my mind, one after the other, a thousand minutely different versions of the thought, I can't believe I'm actually going *through* with this; all the people back home, if they knew, would be shouting, "Oh, no, get ahold of yourself, nothing is *making* you do this."

But even now, looking up into that same sky, I find peace in repeating, "Never mind." It still works. "Never mind."

Orange buoy, smaller than a basketball. I'm not the last to arrive, and I draw strength from this. We all bob in the water. Adrian asks if I'm okay; I ask if she is. We're nodding. Juan reviews the instructions first seen on the pink sheet.

Nodding and nodding, an aeon of nodding.

I remove and spit onto the inside of my mask, rub the saliva around, rinse it off, which prevents fogging.

This is it.

"Um," I ask, "will it be any harder to pull air through the breathing tube at one hundred and thirty feet?"

Juan shakes his head. "No, the regulator takes care of that. It'll feel the same."

Good old Juan. Good old everyone.

I hit the BC's yellow button over my collarbone, and air hisses as it exits its sacks.

The first few feet under, I learn how wrong I've been; nothing has prepared me for this soft violet light. I am not cold and the view is clear through tons of still water. I'll agree to put those tons on top of me; why should that be a problem?—because *look* at me, hanging with the other five experts in our inexact circle, hanging and falling at once, and I'm not afraid, not afraid. Adrian and I keep giving each other the thumbs-up.

Down over there's the white, sandy bottom, all right, sloping at its appointed forty-five degrees; we're out beyond it, though, dropping even faster, feetfirst into nothing, nothing which isn't inky at all but only a richer shade of violet, richer and richer the deeper I am able, sinking, to look. Like the sky, it's disastrous, it's a comfort, takes me in, snuffs every quickflare of panic that releases in my chest before it can burn my cool brain.

Suddenly, we're level with the top of the wall, at the brink of the sandy slope, then it's rising past our masks, maybe fifteen feet away, right *there,* this notorious cliff, but *look*—it's merely pitted stone with here and there a muted, leafy sprout of cabbage-green coral.

On a lark, I try glancing to the base.

Below my flippers already, they jut, those stalactites, mounted simple and fat on the overhang this wall leads down to. Cousteau and his team discovered them twenty-two years ago, and yet here they are themselves, and here am I myself, and it hits me: You mean, I *get* to go *touch* them?

Wheeee!

Hey, let's check the depth gauge.

Ninety feet!

Chicken feed!

Gleeee!

With the press of a button (adding a blast of air to my BC), copying the others, I stop my descent, hold still beside a grand stalactite, thicker than any tree, crusty with barnacles, tapering to a dull point under me. I reach out and brush the rough hide with my fingertips.

"Look where we *are*, Buddy," I say in bubbles.

Juan is doing his job, checks us all by means of an inquiring thumbs-up; we pump ours in return.

The six of us are in a superslow-motion dream ballet but scarcely in reference to one another. Adrian is off to my left, staring into the shade under the ceiling, where the word *inky* does begin to apply. Two men venture in there, swim among the sparse-forest stalactites, but not so far that I lose sight of them. I believe that's Gordon with the flashlight and camera. I consider following them, but I decide instead to look up.

Oh.

oh

How to believe the surface is so far—glittering pale silver, and the sun, so tiny, silver as well, trembling beyond it—and so strictly *rationed,* choked off, bounded by the dark curvature of the near rim, which takes up most of my field of vision? Although I can see only a small arc of the whole circle—the rest erased by refracted light—this much insists that I am way, *way* down inside a crater, and that my entire warm and colorful world is available, anymore, only through a *portal.*

Three more panic-flares go off, and I want to cry. I close my eyes. Never mind. That world up top will wait, and if I am honest, can I say I'm desperate to return?

I hear a clanking. Ten feet above me, Juan's rapping a knife against his tank to get my attention. With his hand, he orders me *up.* I've gone too low. My gauge reads one hundred thirty-five feet. I obey the man.

It's almost time to go.

BCs have pockets, one on each side, that close by means of Velcro. I open my right pocket and pull out Brigid's shirt, the turtleneck from last night. I hold it in both hands, by the shoulders, take a good look, then I fold the collar over in half carefully. I remove the regulator from my mouth and kiss the collar, say into it, "Never mind, Buddy."

I suck the regulator back into my mouth and release the shirt. The two stones (from the hotel's garden) that I've tied into the left sleeve work like charms. I watch it going away beneath me, a mossy clump led by that sleeve into the dense, enclosing violet. And then, before it's entirely gone, I stop looking.

Unfortunately, Juan's seen it too, and so has Adrian. Slightly above me and maybe ten feet away, he points down. I give him the thumbs-up, all I can think to do. He taps Adrian, beside him, on the shoulder; they look at each other; he raises his palms and she raises her palms back, shrugging.

For a moment, I expect Juan to zoom down after it, angry that I've littered, but he does not.

We ascend, and although I wasn't aware of being chilly, a remarkable warmth greets us as we crest the wall and begin slowly to make our way up the shining hill of sand. Adrian reaches out and shakes my hand. Several times, the group pauses, because it's important to give the body time to rid itself of built-up nitrogen.

A jellyfish the size of a popover has gotten flipped onto its back; Juan pokes it lightly with a stick, tries to right it, fails. I touch an ash-colored sponge that has many bulbous prongs to it. Its rubber-ball surface gives under my fingers.

I want to scream out, so proud of myself. Everything's sunny and languorous here, suddenly no hurry, all of us spread out upon this reward-field. I wish we could stay.

We encounter an odd tribe: pencil-thin black eels, hundreds of them, sticking up out of holes, one for each, and modestly swaying, mouths open. They are six inches tall, at least the part they show, and at least until I come close, at which point they scrupulously withdraw. Several times, I attempt to touch one, but the head of my target disappears at the last instant. As soon as I begin, myself, to retreat, he emerges and grows taller at the very same pace, and so do the others in his vicinity. I try sneaking up many times, but it's no use; they are professionals.

Back in the boat, I tell Juan and Adrian that that was my lucky shirt and that it fell out of my pocket by mistake. Adrian says, "Thank God, I was terrified. At first, I thought it was a person."

Lunch is served on Half Moon Cay, a breezy island maybe a football field wide, twice that in length.

After helping myself to lavish round yawns and devouring piece after piece of cold spicy chicken, piles of refried beans with rice, slices of watermelon, after chugging a bottle of Fanta orange soda, I let Juan lead me with the others along palm-lined pathways to the other side of the island, where there is a booby bird sanctuary with a twenty-foot tower; on its observation deck we are surrounded by treetop nests, can watch these large white boobies tending to outlandishly cottony young, and frigate birds, too, in their own nests, with their own young. At each of their throats hangs a bright red sack, limp and wattlish, which balloons swiftly when they pitch back their heads.

What I loved best, though, happened as we first stepped off the boat and onto this beach. Of all things, a *puppy* rushed up to me, wiggled, jumped against my legs! He must've belonged to the boy who helps take care of the island. I crouched to let him lick my face all over, welcome me back into the world. Adrian snapped a picture.

shadow

Thirty-six hours later—my last evening in Belize. I'm sitting on the dirt, in silence, among tall pines, in the middle of the Mountain Pine Ridge, back on the other side of the country. The sun will be down in minutes.

All day, wending west in my tiny blue rental car, my chest has been light, light, light, my body as gravity-free as if underwater, round-breaths growing in me as ripe and ready to take as these broad flowers bountiful on both sides of the road. So I am brand-new, then? Not so fast. All this is partly due to the fact that a major cold front passed through last night, leaving in its wake temperatures and humidity in the low seventies.

I have walked perhaps a hundred yards, to get where I'm sitting, along a trail that extends beyond the end of the wide dirt landing strip next to Blanceneaux Lodge. Four or five times a year, Francis Ford Coppola flies in here, often with his family; he owns the place; it's his retreat.

I've escaped out to these woods to ask Brigid, "So what next?"

Nothing.

Gnats bump my face.

"Look, after all this, can't you tell me *any*thing?" I'm tired, feel like crying, and these gnats . . .

I remember where I am, and I think, Hey, Sofia Coppola has landed here, and then I remember what good fun Brigid made of her performance in *The Godfather: Part III*. She's exquisitely bad throughout the film, of course, but I'm hearing Brigid's takeoff on her last word, after she's fatally shot on the steps, just before she collapses: "Dad." But she says it with this valley-girl accent, which Brig accentuated, like "D'yawld," or however you'd spell it. It cracked me and our friend Heidi up, as we left the theater that night; she threw lots of variation into it: "D'yawld, can I borrow the car"; "D'yawld, I'm not filling rill gret."

I crack up now too, shake my head with unexpected pleasure.

Another first-time memory. Brigid was just simply so much fun, *made* such fun of people and things. I've realized it again and again: without her on hand, the world and its people *are* getting away with murder.

I glance to my left, and there, about ten feet off and down close to the ground—a small, circular spiderweb. The sun, setting behind it, rainbows its threads.

I crawl over and sit there, hunch to stare. The tiny black creator beats a retreat, tucks herself up above, where a hefty blade of grass, which forms the top beam, curls to provide an enclosure. I wait. She won't come out.

The structure is complete in general, its major contours marked out, girders drawn across the circle, as in a pie graph. The spider has been working from the outermost edge in toward the center, laying silver string from girder to girder all the way around and then starting a little farther in and making another circle, very close to the first one. So far, she's made it approximately one-third of the way toward the center.

As long as I keep staring like this, scrutinizing every detail, she will not resume building; I can see her up inside the curled blade, clenched, packed away.

I get up and walk for miles, down a winding dirt road and back. I pick up and pocket a small stone like a blunt and lumpy arrowhead; on one side, right in the middle, a red dot.

It's after ten, dark outside, and I'm in bed, my head and shoulders propped on clothing and pillows, the big, red three-ring binder in my lap, open to the last few of her letters. Even then I'll have read fewer than one-third of the total. I'm saving the rest. The only light is from a candle on the bedside table. Below me, voices and music.

Tomorrow I fly home and Joy will meet me in Hartford. When I first arrived at Blanceneaux this afternoon, I thought I'd like to take her here, even though it's a cheesy place—cool jazz floats from speakers; the very rich sit with cocktails in Adirondack chairs on decks overlooking the river; and placed throughout the immaculate grounds, for these guests, primitive cabanas with palm-thatched roofs, log walls, air conditioners. Joy and I could honeymoon inside that one, there. She's been softening, lately, on the notion of building a life with me, even on having a child someday.

Yes, I want to step out of the shadow! I want to find my way home.

Ever since I left behind the shade inside the Blue Hole, an

Annie Dillard passage has been on my mind, from the very end of her essay "Total Eclipse":

> When the sun appeared as a blinding bead on the ring's side, the eclipse was over. The black lens cover appeared again, back-lighted, and slid away. At once the yellow light made the sky blue again . . . the real world began there. I remember now: we all hurried away. We were born and bored at a stroke. We rushed down the hill. We found our car; we saw the other people streaming down the hillsides; we joined the highway traffic and drove away.
>
> We never looked back. It was a general vamoose, and an odd one, for when we left the hill, the sun was still partially eclipsed— a sight rare enough, and one which, in itself, we would probably have driven five hours to see. But enough is enough. One turns at last even from glory itself with a sigh of relief. From the depths of mystery, and even from the heights of splendor, we bounce back and hurry for the latitudes of home.

As I was returning, earlier, from my long walk, Amber, the lodge manager's daughter, came up the driveway to ask if I'd seen her cat. I was struck by the way she put it. She said, "In your wanderings, did you happen to see my cat? He's black. He's only six months old, but he's getting older now, and he's been out for twenty-four hours straight."

"I'm sorry, no, I didn't. But I'm going back to the woods to take pictures and I'll keep looking."

"Thanks. His name is Shadow. If you do see him, please tell him to come home."

In her letter of May 2, Brigid tells me she'll be taking a quilting class. "We will make a little wall hanging . . . good to start with, given how much wall we have at home."

MAY 5 ends, "Even at this hour [1:15 A.M.], the people of Barre Street make peculiar, aggressive noises. I seem to hear hammering, or angry feet on a porch, stomping. Please come home."

I've got two more left. Reading these letters has been such a surprisingly uncomplicated, happy thing to do. I defer these last for a minute and take out the *Popol Vuh* for the first time since that night in San Ignacio. I flip to the last section, and find that creation seems well under way; human beings have finally gotten it right; they are fit as fiddles, establishing "houses" everywhere:

> They left their mountain place behind. They sought another mountain where they could settle. They settled countless mountains. . . . Our first mothers and our first fathers multiplied and gained strength at those places. . . .
>
> The number of great houses only reached three, there at the Bearded Place. There were not yet a score and four great houses. . . . And it was . . . there that they began feasting and drinking over the blossoming of their daughters. This was the way those who were called "The Great Houses" stayed together. They drank their drinks and ate their corn there . . . only happiness in their hearts when they did it. They ate, they feasted inside their palaces.
>
> And then they got up and came to the citadel of Rotten Cane. . . . And they built many houses there. . . . After that their domain grew larger; they were more numerous and more crowded.

What Brigid reminds me of next, however, plunders this sunny progress:

> *I think you should know that I still perceive this whole marriage thing as a threat, and that it's pointless for you to take that personally. I have lots of good reasons for feeling threatened . . . by an . . . institution which was never designed to suit the needs of women as individuals seeking to achieve. You sometimes act as though you want me to feel as you feel, and sometimes you seem to want me not*

to rock the boat, or to crimp your fantasy. But I have to tell you that this will never be easy for me; this is not a rite of passage I feel safe undergoing, because the passage I will enter is fraught with difficulty, not just because I am female, but because of my character, which is weak and fearful. . . . I am right to be afraid. And if you aren't, well, you're lucky.

I don't want to ruin the truth through reduction; I know that an unproblematic "back home" never was for us. Taking herself seriously meant taking seriously how genuinely difficult it was to do so. I hate myself for ever causing her to feel like a killjoy.

The thing that heartens me, as I read and read looking for little insights or models or bits of wisdom, is that when I read about a marriage that seems to have worked, it seems to me that you and I have the ingredients. We're friends, and we love each other. We respect each other, and we love to converse. . . . But I think what I crave, and the thing which would most help me get married, is a promise on your part to honor my ambitions, and to do your best to help me realize them.

Did I ever make that promise? I mean make it in a huge, clear, unforgettable manner? I do not remember. I want to go back and make it. I want to go back.

I take from the table the stone I found today and hold it in my palm, study its shape. Of course it is Vermont, roughly, and the bloodred dot (which doesn't wash off) marks our life, our house, where we spent our last four years' worth of short and long days.

May 10, 1991

Dear Christopher,

This will be my very last letter to you this spring, the end of this phase of grief and crankiness. I really will miss writing you letters, though. It has been a joy to count on you writing, to save up thoughts for you, to contemplate how to tell you about my days without you, and to plan out how to make you laugh, off in your little piney realm. I picture you . . . stepping irregularly down that windy dirt road into the tree-shadow, your head bent down over what I send you, smiling to yourself, and laughing sometimes, giving a floppy stomp of the foot once in a while when I've really gotten to you. I love to think of it, and hope that it's truly that way. Even though I miss you terribly, I hope we will always have some chances to write each other, because I don't think there is any wooing as real for writers as that which takes place on paper. But you know, another thing I've been picturing pretty cheerfully, with a certain bee-like satisfaction, is when we put our letters together in a box and label it, and put it away. This has been a very pleasing correspondence; we will put it up like vegetables and get it down again when the world is bleak and we're hungry for how things were just now. Maybe we'll have some puling brats who will like to chew over all this, who will struggle to read it all in the order, back and forth, in which it was written and read. Perhaps one of us will die young, in which case I suggest lining the coffin with these letters; what could be more comforting for the dead one than that? This was a good time in our life together to be writing.

Your letter of the 8th arrived today, and fit so well with what I'd been writing to you; it gave me a lot of solace. It will sound so ridiculous to you, but I have to say it: your acknowledgement of my equality, your support of my desire for a sane life with more writing in it, is the most important thing you can give me . . . one thing I've always loved about you is the basic fact that you want to support me. . . .

On the way to City Hall [this evening, to meet friends], I felt very good, by the way. I felt comfortable and solid, and like you and I have been getting to the kind of understanding I've really wanted. The vehemence of what you said on the phone today was great: sell the house if necessary, quit the office. . . . I felt, for the first time in a while, consciously in the stream of life as a person, a woman, walking down the street and feeling possibilities, limits, years past and years coming on me. It was a beautiful evening, sunny, with a dark bruisey sky off to one side, cars wheeling by, the grass so green, and a little blow in the air.

(Before I left the spiderweb, I tried to get an even *better* look by putting my hand behind it, to block out the sun, which was glaring in my eyes. As soon as I did, the web completely disappeared.)

I will be so happy to see you, and to be bringing you home. I have some wonderful new books to show you.

Brigid has no stone or marker; I've never even seen her ashes, don't know where or how they're kept. At one point, before she burned up, I was asked if I'd like to have a lock of her hair, but I said no, figuring that—since true substance was taken —most sense was made by a clean break with all trappings of substance.

I heard of a woman whose daughter's face was smashed in a car wreck and who spent hours in the hospital with her carefully, carefully combing all the blood out of her long blond hair.

I am standing here on a flat rock that rests at the bottom of the frogpond, *my* frogpond; this water I haven't touched for twenty-seven years seems shallower and much stiller than before, rising only to my midcalves, cool, dark, and algae free. I arrived just minutes ago, and already it's clear that the frogs are all gone. I'd hoped to find them still crouched statuelike but painfully alive at all the old spots around this shoreline; these trees have grown taller, denser, shutting out the sunlight from above, stopping plant life, cycles of growth and decay, and thus the small insects my frogs used to eat. I swish my feet around, even shove one far down into the chilly muck beside this rock. The water is oddly blank. Only now and then, slight movement: one of those long-legged skeeters flicking its way across the surface.

So what *happened*? What, actually? What? The question won't stop returning. I'm still missing some kernel of whatness. Is it available?

These five months, since my last night in Belize, I have tried without succeeding to crawl out of the shadow and start weaving life again, feel at home in the ordinary daylight.

It's eighty-five degrees in this shade, midafternoon, humid, and from all around me in the woods, that metallic rasp of summer bugs, like when I was five and six, standing on this same rock, and like back there at the edge of the rain forest.

This is the last stop in a weeklong trip my mother and I have taken, to visit all the places we lived in my earliest years. She's dropped me off here, has gone to lunch with old friends.

We drove first to Chicago, where we found the brick apartment building in which I was conceived, March 1960. The story goes that my mother had just returned from the funeral of a young woman who'd died of a bacterial infection less than twenty-four hours after scratching a pimple on her back; her husband, a doctor, couldn't save her.

It happened that night, my mother expansive with thoughts of life's briefness, the intertwining of love and death.

We visited the University of Chicago's Lying-in Hospital, walked down the long, empty hallways in what used to be the birthing area, though she couldn't locate the very room, or the one where she first held me, where she cried inconsolably because she knew I was going to grow up and leave her.

But look now, it's thirty-three years later, and I'm still here; we can spend eight days in a car together, talking, just sitting quietly, or reading aloud from Mom's old daily record book. We're each thankful to be taking this trip together, that the other *wants* to.

April 16, 1965: C. said he loved me so much he couldn't untouch me.
Feb. 24, 1967: He gives me looks and says, Am I thinking the same thing you are?

After Chicago, we traveled east again, to Madison, New Jersey, to Wendell Hall on the campus of Drew University, the scruffy graduate student dormitory where I was a one-year-old, and then to the apartment in town, 6 Park Avenue, where I was two and three.

The street-level door was open, luckily, so we climbed the steep staircase to the first-floor hall, the same dingy brown-and-white linoleum tiles leading to what used to be the Doyles' door and, across from it, our own brown door.

It takes your breath away, makes you feel faint and kind of regretful, to clap your eyes for the first time in three decades onto sights—this staircase, this short, L-shaped hallway—that have been firmly laid into the floor of your mind and are therefore not *supposed* to be floating free out in the world anymore, in everyday three-dimensional space. There's a kind of obscenity to it, this casual exhibition of the sacred.

I knocked on our door—nobody home—and checked to make certain it was locked.

Back down the stairs we went, and across the street, to a little grassy area with trees.

"I'm not sure, but I *think* this is the one," my mother said, placing her palm on the rough bark of a medium-sized oak. I touched it too, even patted it chummily, though of course I didn't want to believe that this, so ordinary and generally available, could be the tree itself. Hundreds of cars and trucks and pedestrians have passed within inches of it every day, since the night I struck it with my snowball; others have struck it with theirs.

Standing here in the pond, I notice that my forehead is sore, the muscles inside it that I use for concentrating. Yesterday and today, riding and walking through this ancient landscape, my brain has felt like an extremity that's fallen asleep and is only beginning to get those remotest pins-and-needles of waking up, no real blood returning yet; I've been caught napping and shaken, again and again, by quick, never-forgotten displays, tricksters on all sides; but I can't say I exactly *remember* them either: the chestnut tree where my mother used to take me to gather the green-spined balls, where we went, early, the day my sister Becky was born; quick glimpses up long streets, around corners, up the worn brick sides of buildings; and then, outside town, those twists in the road, this certain plunge-down-and-to-the-left under trees, unremarkable yet crucial, on the way out to

Martins Creek on Route 611; the wide, chalky smokestacks, on
the right, of Paterson Bros. Cement Factory. These images and
dozens of others have gone to form basic contours of my mind;
I can tell I've never done without them since the start of thinking, am vaguely aware that they accompany all my ideas, capricious pictures pretending to illustrate, perfectly, notions even so
broad as "all day," "breathing," "out," "*spending* money,"
"that's right," "hope so."

In Martins Creek, just now, before the pond, I walked over a
narrow bridge beside an empty, square-cornered field, and I
suddenly knew that this field has humbly shown itself every
single time, year after year, I have thought, Believe me. So *this* is
"believe me."

I stamped the blacktop hard with my sneakers and said, as of
old, "I'm on the earth; I'm *standing* on the planet Earth."

It turned out the house we lived in isn't, mostly, made of stone;
only the back part is, one room, about a third of its total length;
the rest is white clapboard. The woman who now owns it carried
a baby on her hip when we pulled into the driveway, was preg-
nant with another. We hadn't called ahead, started explaining
ourselves as soon as we stood out of the car.

I didn't tell her everything, of course, but she said I should
feel free to look around, to go and walk in the woods, take my
time. Mom drove away, and the owner went back in what
used to be the Kecks' house, the place where the kitten I buried
in the mud probably grew up and, fifteen years ago, died of advanced age.

I didn't go inside my house or even stand nearer than ten feet;

252 • Christopher Noël

I couldn't see much through the windows—dark inside. But that didn't matter: Here, this little building, this rough yard, and those woods back there, this was the birthplace of my love of the world and what moves within it, and of a thousand particulars about me.

Two hard-boiled eggs in a bowl, brought to me in my room, upstairs, in there, by my father. I have the flu and he's asked what sounds edible. He is a stranger to the kitchen, but my mother is at work. After he shuts the door again, I peel and bite into the first egg; it's undercooked, yolk runny, nauseating. I cannot possibly tell him, and I cry, but I later learn that the Gumby feeling is fundamental, not fluky—this ache caused by failed generosity, like a very humble nostalgia that suddenly spreads its wings over all of us, dooms our feeble gestures.

I've come "home," as directed by my last night in Belize. And although this unprecedented forehead strain means I haven't fit right in, means there's a gap between me and me, I feel, anyway, found again, founded, landed here in this defunct pond water, taken back up and held by my own whole, visible life. Little boy again, maybe I can be, now that I must, at my oldest.

I don't recall feeling confused or shaky or unheroic when last I dedicated myself to this pond, same size (sixty by fifteen), same smells of death and life mashed together. No, I was a searcher for life then, for what's most real; I stalked and pounced on it; I came up with it and held on tight. Under every stone I discovered something worthwhile, trying to escape me; if I saw a likely stone, I couldn't bear *not* to lift it.

• • •

Out of the white cardboard envelope I pull the first of the pictures I have obtained from the Berlin, Vermont, Police Department, from an Officer Leary, who told me he remembers this accident very well. "In my three years here," he said, "I've only had two fatals." He was at least six foot four, pasty Irish face.

"Not fifteen minutes before, I overheard another officer calling in on the radio from his cruiser that conditions were terrible and that we better send salt and sand trucks over there right away."

He himself went to the scene and began taking pictures, but after the first one, he said—the one I now hold in my hand— his camera jammed, froze up. The rest (which he has Xeroxed for me in black-and-white) were sent over, later, by the newspaper photographer. Before I left his office, I shook his hand.

Officer Leary must have climbed the snowy hillside next to Route 2, because the shot is from above. Gray, snow-dusted road surface, then bright snowcover off both sides of the two-lane highway, and there's our little Honda, good old car, hello again, powder blue, plain as day, sitting crosswise in the near lane, a station wagon and a pickup being directed past in the other lane. From this angle (straight-on) it's tough to make out the full damage to the driver's side, though I can see it has been caved in. The driver herself isn't here anymore; the passenger doors and the driver's-side back door have been forced open, and the ambulance isn't here anymore either. A police cruiser is parked fifteen feet away on the road, and ten feet this side of our car, roughly perpendicular to it, seeming twice its size, tilted into a ditch, a red and white Chevy Blazer (not a Ford Bronco after all). Six uniformed men, police and rescue personnel, stand in pairs, talking. The pair closest to our car regards it studiously. The man (I think it's a man) who is passing in the pickup is also looking.

Only now is this accident definitely not a rumor.

The second picture is large (six by nine?) and, for a Xerox, extremely sharp. This time, we're at ground level and sighting along the road, Blazer off to the left, Honda to the right. Here it's much earlier; lots of commotion. Back home, I'm probably still in bed. Twelve men surround our car, many with MFD— Montpelier Fire Department—on the backs of their coats, three of them working at Brigid's door. They're blocking my view of her. Curlicuing over the ice on the shoulder, leading from what looks to be a generator over to the hidden place in front of the three men, a thick cord that I assume powers the "jaws of life." The other nine men are watching those three and, standing by on the other side of this whole knot, *two* ambulances.

I pick my eyes up off that frantic January surface already over thirty months past and give them back to the deep hush of warm leaves shimmering all around me and my pond. Except for some weakness in the knees, I feel surprisingly sturdy, ready for this. Is it providing the "kernel of whatness"? Well, *some* of it, if not the *kernel* of the kernel. Since I'm peculiarly still hungry, it's at least more for me to gnaw and swallow.

I've been so scared of this day, have told myself to let go of the idea; yet I've also been looking forward—as if to Christmas morning—to finally getting a look at these pictures. I'd hoped to find in them the spectacular kid herself—"Oh, *there* you are" —wedged inside our car all lonely and surprised; and then I could fit myself in beside her where I belong. I could see her through.

The woman in the Blazer never responded to the letter I wrote her six months ago, and the other woman—the one who was supposed to have stopped at the scene and held Brigid's hand— never got her letter because she turned out not to *exist*, to have emerged, instead, from talk, as in the game of telephone, a new coin from the pocket of a verbal hand-me-down.

Therefore, I recently made contact with the nurse who sent the letter I put at the beginning of this book. And then, the day before Mom and I left for Chicago, I met her at a Montpelier bakery and café. She's about forty, maybe forty-five, with long, curly brown hair and thick glasses, a mild face and a very informal manner, good-humored, easy to talk to. We shook hands, and I bought her a scone and a cup of coffee; myself, I had a lemon Danish and a decaf.

She praised me for my courage in phoning her, said she appreciated it since she's sent many such letters to families and has never once heard back from them. I told her that she was famous in mine not only for having been with Brigid when we couldn't be, acting as our stand-in, but for having taken the time to tell us about it.

Then I asked, "Can you take me through the experience from your point of view?" She readily agreed to let me record her, and in the background, on the tape, one can hear the clinking of

cups, saucers, silverware, and the rise and fall of Tuesday afternoon chitchat, though I wasn't aware of it at the time.

Um, yeah, we knew she was coming before she came because
she was entrapped in the car, so we were getting periodic updates
on her condition as the EMTs worked on her, to get her out of
the car. We knew it was bad, just from the mechanism of injury
—as we call it—and the extended period of extrication. And they
did a bang-up job getting her out and getting her to us as well as
they did.

*How many minutes would you say it was from the time of the
accident?*
Thirty to forty. Well, from the time of the accident I don't
know . . . it was a good thirty-five minutes from the time they got
called and were on scene until we had her. That's much too long.
But it was amazing that they got her there as well as they did. Sort
of controlled chaos in what we call the trauma code room, the
room that's set up to handle essentially everything. . . . I remember
when she first came in having to assess her full condition rather
than just the obvious injuries. She had, for example, an open
fracture on her right ankle, open just means there was a little hole
in her skin, there wasn't bone sticking out or anything. But that
could have been overlooked. I remember clearly our physician
assistant was down there splinting and wrapping that ankle while
everybody was working on everything else.

Did somebody yell at him or her?
No, somebody told him to do it. You had to do that because
pain increases the shock, so we want to splint anything that might
be causing her more pain.

So there was no consciousness involved?
I don't recall her ever being conscious. She was responsive early
on, to pain. I talked to her, to tell her what we were doing, but

that's automatic at that point, particularly for nurses, and for some physicians: there's going to be a poke in your arm right now, I'm starting an IV, you need to hold still. We say that automatically. She did flinch at pain a couple of times, as I recall. A lot of tests were done right away, portable X rays . . .

That's how you found out the spleen was . . . I remember being told the spleen was . . .

Yeah, well, we did what's called the belly tap, which is just a little tube into the side to see if there's free fluid in there. There was; that's why we had to go to the OR. We drew blood, which is an immediate thing to do when we're starting IVs, so we typed and crossed her, tried to, I think she ended up getting O blood anyway, the first unit or two, 'cause we didn't have time to cross her, just typed her, um, that's all technical stuff. We had to get blood into her, we did, we were pushing fluids . . .

So she had the universal donor?

Yeah, yeah, we had pressure bags on the IVs, so the fluid would go in, because her blood pressure was *extremely* low.

Right, she must have had to have the "trousers" [inflatable pants that squeeze the legs, increase the blood pressure in the rest of the body] at a certain point . . .

Mmmm hmmm, I think she came in with them on, which did help splint her some. Um, did a chest tap, did a belly tap, the chest was negative, the belly was positive. Pushing fluids into her. Hmmm, she came back from X ray. She went to the OR, I remember running down the hall with her, one of the few times it's like the movies. In the movies they always run down the hall. Typically, we do not run, we can walk fast, but you've got all these poles, the IVs, if you smash the IVs it doesn't do anybody any good. Um . . . the operation was really quick and really thorough. I read the surgical report, they did a nice job. Had to remove the spleen. It was, they said, not just torn or something, but basically broken in half.

Oh, so they removed it? *I was told, I think I was told, that they'd sewn and put it back together, but that's not true.*

No, it came out in pieces. And the bed that it was in, you know, the area around it, was all closed off so it would stop bleeding, packed, sewn up. And then she just went right back out to get in the ambulance. . . . Um, the anesthesiologist went with us. At that time she was intubated . . .

"Intubated" means what?

Tube into her lungs, to breathe for her.

That's right. I remember an episode of Rescue 911 *where some guy intubated without—*

Without permission, yeah I saw that too! Oh, give me a break, that's going to be a real problem for you, buddy.

Why, is it not usually a big deal to do that?

Well, it is, but if you know how to do it and somebody needs it, you don't agonize over it.

They were trumping it up for TV purposes.

Well, you know everybody on *911* lives, unless they're an organ donor! [laughs.] So, I talked with Eric definitely before we left, I think while she was in surgery, trying to explain a few things, and the plan was she would go to Burlington, 'cause of her head injury.

And based on the CAT scan, did anybody give her much of a chance at that point?

Um, yeah, we had some hope. Wasn't a lot, you know. But we were fixing the things that could be fixed, and at that point, you know you can't really assess a head injury that quickly.

'Cause things swell?

Yeah, and we were doing everything we could to keep it from swelling. We, before she went to the OR, gave her Mannitol, which is an intravenous diuretic, which helps lower the pressure in the brain. We had her intubated and were hyperventilating her, which lowers the carbon dioxide content, and blows that off, which keeps the swelling down. It doesn't get rid of what's already there, but it prevents it from getting worse quicker.

Right, the rate . . .

Yeah. So she's intubated and on the way, and we had respiratory therapy bagging her on the ride. I was the RN and Dr. Z was the anesthesiologist . . . and we made *very* good time, one of the quicker trips. We went Code 3, which is lights and sirens, and boogie.

Officer Leary gave me the photographs for free, but the police report cost fifteen dollars. On the first page, at the top right: *Accident #007.* Seventh of the new year. All down the page, boxes are filled in. Operators' dates of birth: *4/10/29* and *3/17/65;* estimated speeds: *Chevy Blazer, 45 mph; Honda Civic, 40 mph;* seat belt code 5: *both drivers wearing belt and harness;* injury codes: *3 (non-incapacitating);* and *1 (fatal).*

On the next page is a diagram showing the road and two simple rectangles, repeating, at different stages of progress. After going straight two rectangles' worth, Vehicle 1's third appearance shows it all the way over in the other lane, nearly facing the opposite direction; an arrow connecting the second and third drawings indicates the slide and spin. Vehicle 2's smaller rectangle moves northeast. Its second drawing has it angled slightly to the right because the larger rectangle is in its way now. In the last two depictions, both rectangles rest where the cars in the photographs are.

Page 3:

Upon arrival I found the following: both vehicles were on the south side of the road. Vehicle #2 was straddling the breakdown lane and facing south. Vehicle #1 was off the roadway surface and facing west. The operator of Vehicle #2 (CLARK) was trapped in her vehicle and had to be removed by a Fire Department Rescue Team. . . . Both operators had suffered injuries and were transported to Central Vermont Hospital by the Montpelier Ambulance Service. It appeared that CLARK was bleeding from the head and had suffered severe head injuries. [The other driver] complained of a sore/hurt right chest. In talking with the witnesses and the operator of Vehicle #1 it appears that the following had occurred:

VEHICLE #1: The operator advised that she was traveling west (toward Montpelier) on Route 2. As she approached the accident area she believed that her vehicle struck an icy patch on the roadway and started to skid. She stated that she thought the vehicle started to skid to the right, she corrected and the next thing she remembered was being in the east-bound lane (opposite from her direction of travel) and being struck by another vehicle. She then remembered the vehicle coming to rest on the shoulder of the roadway and partially in a ditch.

VEHICLE #2: The operator was transported to Central Vermont Hospital and then to the Medical Center Hospital of Vermont, in Burlington. At 1620 hours Officer Leary spoke with Dr. B.W. [the Medical Center Hospital Medical Examiner], she advised that Ms. Clark had been pronounced dead as of 1415 hours, 01/28/92 by the Emergency Room Staff. The initial cause of death (prior to autopsy) was from "Closed Head Injury—Major Brain Damage" probably due to rapid deceleration.

Page 4:

WITNESS #1: Ms. N.A.P. [stated] that it appeared that the operator of Vehicle #2 attempted to swerve to the right to avoid Vehicle #1 but was unsuccessful in this effort and collided with the right rear side of Vehicle #1. She stated that she [N.A.P.] applied her brakes, her vehicle hit some ice, skidded and did a complete 360 skid/circle before coming to rest approximately 5 feet behind Vehicle #2. . . . Ms. P. further stated that she had been traveling at approximately 40 mph and had followed Vehicle #2 since Grossman's Lumber Store.

According to their typed captions, the last three photographs were taken at 9:10 A.M.; back home, I must be up and waiting by the window for Coleen's car, also a blue Honda Civic, to pull up front and get me.

Here on the road, show's over, most everybody's gone, only a few men left, cleaning up from the extraction. One stoops beside two pair of the jaws of life, blunt, muscular pliers the size of jackhammers, lying quiet and off-duty now on the icy ground; he seems to be winding their long cords back up. Three other men inspect the damage, and so can I; for the first time the view is clear and the angle is good. How on earth is such a crushing of Brigid's side possible at forty or forty-five miles per hour? Augmented by the spin of Vehicle 1, its right rear end swinging into her like a pinball paddle? The force, as I've always imagined, is indeed centered exactly at her door; it is punched in so deeply, everything rearranged, that the tire nearest to it points, like a satellite dish, toward the low part of the sky.

On the one hand, this whole affair seems bulky; from her door to the left headlight socket, the metal is bent impossibly like the thick iron bar of a circus strongman.

On the other hand, since all window glass is missing, the car seems like one of those Matchbox models.

In plain sight, from another angle, is my front license plate—NOVEL. I chose it back in 1986, both because it contains my name and to spur me to write my first novel. It used to draw amused comments all the time, but have I thought about it once since this car was scrapped?

In the last picture I can see all the way inside to both front seats. For some reason Brigid's door has been pried open now (though she was missing already in the last two shots, when it hadn't been), so I can float eyes-first into that space—where we spent, all told, weeks together—which has been molded into a new chamber, vaulted, the roof above it crimped up, like a capital **A**. This shot's just slightly out of focus, so I can't make out any blood or objects in here, just the familiar fuzzy fabric of the seats, hers pulled up close to the wheel, where she felt most comfortable.

But my friend Sal and my stepfather, Peter, climbed in later and gathered things, put them into a clean box no larger than a toaster oven's. Sal's been keeping this box for me ever since.

Sinking in with each step, I leave my rock and gingerly cross the sharp and viscous floor, hoist myself up onto the steep bank by grabbing a tree root with my free hand, all the sheets of paper reenveloped in my other. From the top of the bank, a pathway leads out of these deeply frogless shadows and into the sunshine that falls on the railroad tracks.

I've stashed Sal's box here in the foliage. I pick it up, rattle its unguessable contents, not heavy, once again by my ear. I also pick up another envelope, Federal Express, sent to me by our friend Heidi.

Carrying everything I'll need, I start walking along the rail, balancing, toward the trestle. I pass the mossy spot, off to the right, where I sat after burying the kitten, where I let those mosquitoes fill up on my blood and fly away, where I waited for my mother to come get me.

The trestle is a flat bridge over the river, maybe thirty feet long instead of the great span I remember; and the river is only fifteen feet below. But like before, I can look down between the ties and see the water going fast, and this still makes me dizzy.

Halfway across, over the left edge and about six feet below the tracks, a triangular cement shelf sticks out. Laboriously, I get myself and my things down onto it. I peer in under the tracks—the small "room" I used to climb into, where fairies used to live; but the opening, between two girders, is much too narrow for me now, and the steel floor is covered with glass and trash.

I turn, sit cross-legged facing the shallow oncoming river, set the box in front of me, open it. The sunlight is bright and hot here, and the two green license plates glint their white letters: NOVEL.

Next I pull out Brigid's wide, thick beige wool scarf; yes, of course, she wore this every day when it was cold—her most sumptuous scarf. Here and there, dark, crusty spots. Maybe they aren't bloodstains.

A sweater of mine—rust and navy—that I've forgotten all about.

And my maroon gloves; I wondered where they'd gotten to.

A bunch of papers from the glove compartment, including repair receipts and a manila envelope full of directions, in Brigid's handwriting, to various frequent destinations: her parents' new house; her siblings; our friend Matt Goodman in Somerville; my sister Becky and her boyfriend Paul in Watertown. They're married now and live elsewhere.

But it's the last item I'm gladdest to find, her keys, including the one for the car and the two for our house, which, the last time I saw it, had a government sign pasted onto the front door: HUD HOUSE FOR SALE—CONTACT ANY REALTOR.

What's most famous about this key chain, though, what I press in my hands and up against my cheek, what shouts out with lost everydayness, with forms familiar as your thumb yet misplaced a thousand times and found at the last minute, what causes me to gasp at having been separated from them *without knowing it,* are two translucent plastic pieces, one roughly the size and shape of a bar of hotel soap, with her first name engraved all in caps, letters reversed, as in a mirror, so that you have to look from the back, *through* the quarter inch of plastic, in order to read it; and the other, a four-inch, cigar-thick tube filled with water or oil and tiny metal red and silver and yellow stars and moons and suns, and pink sparkly dust, all of which falls in slow motion toward the bottom end if you hold the tube vertical, or, if horizontal, spreads itself gaudily through the entire length.

I realize with piercing disappointment that this long-awaited Christmas morning is almost at an end; there remains, in the envelope, only Heidi's description of visiting the funeral home.

I hate having nothing left open to me but rituals; I also hate running out of them. And of course I hate finishing this book: It does not make any sense, because ever and again, I continue to feel the sensation that made me start it, that of *just having* landed, of that quick sulk in the spine, the modest sinking inside that occurs the moment after one truly stops. And always the brand-new thought, So it's come to *this,* has it?

I will keep circling back, search-party fashion, to the beginnings and endings and middles, back to basics. As Mexican writer Jaime Sabines puts it, "One is never done finding ways to be rid of the dead." Or, I'd add, to greet them.

Leaving Belize, way back in early March, it seemed I'd now be moving on. Everything pointed that way. Amber's lost cat Shadow came home, yowled out front at dawn; I heard him, and heard the girl run from her room and down the stairs to the door, take him in.

Rushing back across the country in my rental car, afraid of missing my return flight to Joy and my new life, I zoomed past two kids by the side of the road, a girl, ten or twelve, leaning down to work on some problem at the rear of her bicycle, which was propped up by its kickstand; and on the seat, upright, unassisted, the tiniest child, tall as a ham, chubby, shirtless, bright black, and holding out in its left hand a length of white cloth that seemed to be lace.

I didn't think I had time to stop and ask to take a picture, and then the scene was gone.

But here's the thing: For miles I kept almost turning back anyway, because the regret at leaving this sight behind, forever, set up such a complicated vibration in the suddenly plentiful strings of my chest and belly that I thought, Oh, look, I'm alive again, fully, must be, because *feel* this. Exquisite strummings, quick, fancy shapes appearing and vanishing inside me, and the *total* absence of rotting cabbage! Missing this bike-seat kid so abundantly cleared room in me for loving everything I would not miss in the future.

Back in Northampton, springtime came, and I breathed like a pro, attaining that yawnish reach-and-grab *anytime I wanted it*, a grant I carried with me, like a kid with a caught creature in his pocket, always checking to be sure of it, finding it thriving.

Like Joy and me. She'd made sure I had food stocked in my refrigerator for my first few exhausted days back home; forget that island puppy, how lucky I was to have *this woman* to welcome me back to the world! We spent most of our free time together; she said I seemed much more solid to her, more reliably "here"; she tapped on my chest when she said this. She stared in my eyes. Our stylistic differences felt manageable. We began hinting around about going ahead with things, finding a place, even, yes, having a child. Onward and upward!

And then it happened, after only three weeks—a sudden loss of cabin pressure. I emptied and tailspun, breathless, out of the sky; she couldn't find me anymore when she stared in my eyes. I took my old job back, sprawled out on bed or couch, staring and rotting, cabbage-man. When I couldn't explain myself, she was furious and stunned. I made flailing attempts, but the best I could muster was "I'm not sure what's the matter, but I don't feel quite right in this relationship anymore." Suddenly our differences seemed decisive to me again. I felt, vaguely, not quite at home; a fringe of nervousness had grown around my heart. I'd felt it before, had been trying to convince myself otherwise, and in so doing I had convinced Joy. Just when she'd started to lower her guard and relax her hard-won suspicions about love, I'd stabbed her in the belly. She said that I was taking the easy way, refusing to climb back into the trenches of regular life, to buckle down to the task of loving an actual-angled, non-Brigid woman. She said, "Go ahead then, there's nothing I can do if you want to be too beautiful for the world."

Make no mistake; everything *is* reduced. As Stanley Keleman puts it, "Big dying evokes little dying."

I have moved back to Montpelier, to the dot on the Vermont stone, and am renting a cheap house in the woods for the fall and winter. Taking a semester's leave from teaching, in order to get somewhere on my novel, I'll be living on the last few hundred dollars from the lawsuit.

Joy is planning to move to Brooklyn.

The body: astonishing to recognize Brigid and know so certainly that it was *not* my Briggie. The casket was enormous, the effect of her body laid a foot down from the head of it being to shrink her. Her head was covered with several white cloths over the top and sides, no hair showing (probably shaved off during surgery). I suppose the wounds were pretty gruesome. So this little person. But her face swollen so large and pale, bruising about the eyes. Her *little* cranium, big face. Mouth open, sneering a bit, with her beautiful front teeth all broken off. I had thought of this detail before we'd come and so it didn't shock—but painful, I felt so tender towards her. She was swaddled all around like a baby. Through the red dress with black splotches I could see a dark brassiere and noticed how *flat* it was—no chest there I'm sure— they put something with her clothes on it over her to hide the damage. Grateful for the lack of cosmetic fiddling otherwise. Amazingly, with all the evident trauma to her body, the scene was very peaceful—really she could have been sleeping if she weren't so breath-takingly absent. I did have the desire to rock her and console her; how useless the feeling.—Heidi Pollard, 2/9/92

After putting everything back into the box and replacing it in the weeds beside the tracks, I cross the trestle and keep going until a sheer slate wall begins to rise on my right. I may have come this far before, but no farther; and I certainly never climbed this narrow pathway here that takes me steeply up the wooded hill above the slate wall and the tracks. When I get to the top, I'm out of breath; the path continues, and I can see a clearing up ahead.

>   *So were you free to talk to her much of the time? Or did you have a lot of other stuff to do?*
>   Interestingly, I had very little to do, because Dr. Z was doing my usual part, which is adjusting medication rates and doing the monitoring and assessing things. . . . So I had more time to talk to her, which felt good.
>
>   *So did you hold her hand?*
>   Yeah. I held her hand, and stroked her arm, you know, those long muscles in the arm, which can be soothing and it's a way to block pain from the short muscle fibers. It's one of those theory things, but if you believe it, it works. I believe it, it works. So I was holding her hand and sitting on her left, so holding her left hand, um, stroking her left arm, talking to her, and primarily just telling her what we were doing, where we were going, what had happened to her, that you were waiting for her, that her parents knew about it, 'cause I think that was important for her to know, that they knew what was going on, and that people loved her, and I told her you loved her several times . . .
>
>   *So Eric told you about me?*
>   Yeah, I knew there was a Chris.

But then were you much involved once you got to Burlington, or you relinquish control?

Technically you do, once you get there. . . . Interestingly enough, Dr. Z did her internship there, so she knew everybody and everyone knew her . . .

She just slid right in . . .

Slid right in, and gave her report, I gave my report, about her medical condition. I made sure—the thing that bothers me about turning a patient over is not having people use her name—so I made sure that they knew her name and then I referred to her by name several times with this one person, I don't even know who he *was,* but he finally got the drift that we were to use her name, so he was calling her by name. And then we stayed. We stayed for a long time, it was like an hour or something . . . and she died while we were on our way back. From the time we left, she was alive, and when we got back to CVH they told us that they had just called recently from Burlington and she had died, and that was really tough, you know, 'cause we walked in having just left her, and knowing it was critical but thinking we were still going to pull it out. . . .

So the reason that in Burlington they recommended strongly that I not go in and see her after she died was that the head wound was so unlovely?

I didn't know they did that.

Yeah, I mean, and I was in such a kind of aimless and feeble condition that I didn't argue. And I didn't even see her in the funeral home.

I don't think it was ugly. I think fluid resuscitation makes you all puffy, and I'm sure her face was not the face that you remember. And that may be just as well. You know, you don't have this other memory to overlay the memories you have over time.

Well, speaking of that, in the other direction, let me just . . . here are some pictures of her.

Oh, she's beautiful.

This is about six weeks before the accident, at that Christmas. And here's when she was like seventeen. . . .
Wow. A beautiful child.

Me and her together. . . . So.
Oh, those are wonderful. She's beautiful.

And this one is for you to keep.
Thank you for this. That was very sweet of you.

And thank you for being the sort of person who wants it. And here is a book of her writing that you may have too.
Oh, that's really wonderful.

I step out into the tall grass of a green field that slopes upward away from me for a long distance with no houses or anything human in sight. What a distinct new place this is—could be anywhere—perched on top of all of my antiquity.

"I feel so good," I announced to my mother, down below, on September 9, 1966, "all fresh inside me like a wind is blowing inside or something is balanced just right in my stomach." Sometimes, it seems that every muscle in me is cocked forever against the chance I might feel quite this way again.

I did get close, though, while hanging inside the Blue Hole, rapt, captive to the point of violet-soaked relaxation. And I'm not sure why, but when I think of Brigid's shirt lying quiet, even this moment, there on that floor, something clicks into place, yes, in my stomach. Have I made her into an organism, real and friendly in the world, whose range extends now to farther than I'll ever go, so that no matter what, I can never leave her behind?

Other times, I feel a subtler progress.

My mother recently mentioned that she was sending back to

Brigid's family a box she'd found in the attic, a box of Brigid's trolls and miniature doll furniture collected as a child, and I was struck most by how this piece of information struck me, as if from slightly off to one side, lateral now instead of looming, as though a hand has swung from noon or midnight to partway down the dial.

Or like a wave that was always hanging over me, ready to cover and drench me, attacks more often only with its spray.

All is slightly drier. For instance, the cabbage still rides in my chest, but now I recognize it by *shape* rather than by putrid weight.

I suppose this is why I am able to meet with the nurse, can look at what I've seen today, and all with this strange pinch of curiosity.

I'm staring at the line that seems drawn, up there, across the farthest visible part of this field. I guess I better admit that it's just such a horizon that suits me best for the time being, a horizon held open, breathable. Don't rush ahead; there is no hurry; enjoy the medium glory of *not yet*.

And what's new? It seems this Castle Keep impulse has been part of me since day one, or, anyway, since February 15, 1966: "I told C. we would rent a cottage on the beach someday and he said I hope not next summer and I said why and he said 'cause then it would be over and I want to save it."

I have to laugh when I see I've written this whole book—more than eighty thousand words—without once breaking through to C. S. Lewis's experience, my mind and Brigid's crisply meeting, unmediated.

But of course it's through language that I can do my best for Brigid, to reach her, to let her reach me; she'd do the same if we traded places. Even if I've spread myself out, here, along only one possible surface of knowing her—this book isn't anything *like* a single snappy glance, a new tug by the arm or a favor or a fight—it's a way of opening my eyes wide and drawing her back down into bed with me on that last morning. Call it an elaborate cuddling method.

It's okay, I've always been made of the same stuff, which is a good comfort. Six weeks before my third birthday, my mother noted that "If I repeat something he says and I say it wrong he says it again the original way and then says, 'That's the way it talks!'"

I take a last glance up at the widespread field, duck back into the forest, and start down toward the tracks.

This is the way it talks.

But one more thing. There is in me what no amount of filibustering can prevent; it plays over and over, the short, simple tune of her. We each have one, don't we? And it's not grand; it's more like a catchy jingle.

She liked to fake dying, to tease me, lying absolutely still at some odd, random moment, and holding her breath, or breathing too secretly for me to tell. This was usually when we'd be in bed in the middle of a conversation. There'd be the pause and the stillness, nothing dramatic, and the pause would drag on, and so I'd say, "Buddy?" I'd join the game, shake her shoulder, keep saying, "Buddy, hey. Buddy?" But pretty soon—it never takes long, though I *know* perfectly well she is alive—I'll find I'm only *pretending* to play along, and she'll detect just the barest edge of anxiety in my voice. That's when she'll start laughing. She will mimic my urgency, show it up: *"Buddy!"* What I don't tell her is that *already,* just then, I was striking up the tune of her in my head, even though she was right here.

About the Author

Christopher Noël lives in Montpelier, Vermont, and teaches in the Master of Fine Arts in Writing program at Vermont College of Norwich University.